I CHING

Andy Baggott

TEACH YOURSELF BOOKS

For UK orders: please contact Bookpoint Ltd, 39 Milton Park, Abingdon, Oxon OX14 4TD. Telephone: (44) 01235 400414, Fax: (44) 01235 400454. Lines are open from 9.00–6.00, Monday to Saturday, with a 24 hour message answering service. Email address: orders@bookpoint.co.uk

For U.S.A. & Canada orders: please contact NTC/Contemporary Publishing, 4255 West Touhy Avenue, Lincolnwood, Illinois 60646–1975, U.S.A. Telephone: (847) 679 5500, Fax: (847) 679 2494.

Long-renowned as the authoritative source for self-guided learning – with more than 30 million copies sold worldwide – the *Teach Yourself* series includes over 200 titles in the fields of languages, crafts, hobbies, business and education.

A catalogue record for this title is available from The British Library.

Library of Congress Catalog Card Number: On file

First published in UK 1999 by Hodder Headline Plc, 338 Euston Road, London NW1 3BH

First published in US 1999 by NTC/Contemporary Publishing, 4255 West Touhy Avenue, Lincolnwood (Chicago), Illinois 60646–1975 U.S.A.

The 'Teach Yourself' name and logo are registered trade marks of Hodder & Stoughton Ltd.

Typeset by Transet Limited, Coventry, England.
Printed in Great Britain for Hodder & Stoughton Educational, a division of Hodder Headline Plc, 338 Euston Road, London NW1 3BH by Cox & Wyman Ltd, Reading, Berkshire.

Impression number	10	9	8	7	6	5	4	3	2	1	
Year		2005	2004	2003	2002	2001	2000	1999			

This book is dedicated to my friend and Tai Chi teacher Simon Suckling.

Acknowlededgments

I would like to thank my partner Debbie Blackaby for her patience and support during the writing of this project and my dear friend Eli Heath for his continued encouragement. Acknowledgement must also go to Les Martin for the information about nuclear hexagrams and Peter Stanton for his input regarding Chinese medicine. Finally thanks to Helen Green and Linda Miles at Hodder & Stoughton for their patience.

CONTENTS

INTRODUCTION

China and the Chinese culture had fascinated me since I was at school. I enjoyed reading Chinese poetry and mythology and greatly admired the early Chinese poets' ability to describe a complex scene or set of emotions with just a few simple words. There was something very attractive about the Oriental way of thinking and their use of metaphor intrigued me. In the 1980s I bought my first copy of Richard Wilhelm's famous translation of the *I Ching* or the *Book of Changes*. I had been attracted to it for two reasons. The first was that it was Chinese and full of short, simple descriptions of people or scenes that were similar to the Chinese poetry I had read. The second was that the cover said that it gave the reader access to ancient Chinese wisdom and I was desperately seeking answers to the problems in my life.

Full of enthusiasm I went straight home and began to read the main text. Within half an hour I was totally confused. The words seemed to make no sense at all. I then decided to read the introduction and learn how to use the *I Ching* for divination. The theory seemed simple enough and I found three coins and asked the oracle a pertinent question about my life. I threw the coins and noted how many heads and tails appeared at each throw. Having worked out which hexagram would contain the answer to my question, I quickly turned to the relevant pages and read. The text talked about the eldest son which was strange because I was the youngest of three boys in my family. Then it talked about thunder and a lake, which seemed to have no relevance to my question at all. Confused and dismayed I abandoned my question and my copy of the *I Ching* was relegated to a bookshelf.

The following year I saw a new translation of the *I Ching* in a bookshop and bought it in the hope that it would help me to better understand this 'great book of wisdom'. I soon found that it offered no insight at all, just more strange metaphors that appeared to have no relation to the questions I was posing. This book, too, was quickly relegated to the bookshelf and was placed next to my Wilhelm *I Ching*.

A few months later I saw Tai Chi lessons advertised in a local newsagent. I telephoned the teacher and arranged to attend the next class. I had no real idea of what Tai Chi was about. I knew it was Chinese and I had seen it performed once and thought it incredibly beautiful. When I arrived at the class there was an atmosphere of peace and calm. As I learnt the first moves to the exercise I had my first sensation of feeling energy in my body. After two hours of Tai Chi, I felt both tired and energized at the same time. For the first time in years I had thought about nothing but what was going on within my own body and it felt good. For two hours I had forgotten all the troubles and cares I had in my life and I had glimpsed freedom.

I practised Tai Chi every day and began to read books about energy and Traditional Chinese Medicine. I began changing my diet and living habits and resolved to study acupuncture. The more I learnt and the more I changed myself, the healthier and happier I felt. I enrolled in acupuncture training and studied a whole host of other therapies. Each year I learnt new things and the more I learnt, the more I changed. Finally I discovered Macrobiotics which is a way of living according to the laws of yin and yang. Through Macrobiotics I learnt about Chinese philosophy and about how to live in harmony and balance with my environment. Life certainly wasn't any easier, but I felt a level of understanding and control in my destiny that I had never felt before. Then one day I was presented with a problem for which I could find no solution. In desperation I decided to consult the *I Ching*. I found three coins and focused my mind on wanting to find a solution to my problem. Once I cast the coins and worked out the appropriate hexagram, I tentatively turned to the relevant pages. As I read the words, the meaning became crystal clear. I was amazed. I understood the metaphors and the answer to my question was so specific that I felt as if it had been written just for me.

It was then that I realized what the *I Ching* really was and how to understand and use it. True wisdom and understanding come not through words, but through experience. I had effected great change in my life and I had actively begun to discover my true path. As I did so, my understanding of the workings of the universe increased and with it my understanding of a book (the *I Ching*) that comments upon the working of the universe increased. The *I Ching* is a very magical book. It is based upon the deep and profound understanding of the workings of the universe by the ancient sages, which are simple and yet infinitely complex. The *I Ching* has the ability to provide commentary and insight into any situation at any time. It comments upon the moment and once its language can be understood, it provides new perspectives that can lead to solutions to problems.

Any problem that you have in your life is only a problem because of the way you are viewing it. If you change your perspective, the problem ceases to exist. For example, I live in a stone farmhouse in the country. To me it is my dream home. I love working outside in the garden and it is quiet and peaceful. It provides the perfect environment for my work as a writer and healer and from my perspective it suits all my needs. To a person who likes living and working in a city, my house would be a terrible place to live. It requires regular maintenance, the nearest town is several miles away and there's not even a village pub. It is all a matter of perspective. If you want to truly understand the *I Ching*, you have to understand yourself and to learn to embrace the only constant that exists in the universe – change. If you actively seek to be happy, healthy and fulfilled, you will naturally find your destiny and with it a deeper understanding of life and the universe.

The *I Ching* will not 'work' for you until you are actively seeking to become more in harmony with the universe around you. This means that you need to seek harmony within yourself. Every negative that you perceive has an equal and opposite positive side if you change your perspective. Seek happiness, health and fulfilment and the *I Ching* will become your friend and ally. Seek to exert selfish power over others or to lie and deceive, and the *I Ching* will reveal nothing to you because the *I Ching* is a book of truths. If you are searching for truth, the *I Ching* will help you to find it. If you are living in delusion, the *I Ching* will offer only frustration and confusion.

This book is divided into two parts. The first part consists of five chapters. The first chapter provides a brief history of divination in China, shows how the 64 hexagrams of the *I Ching* were created and introduces the imagery and relevance of each individual line of a hexagram. The second chapter provides an introduction to the theory of yin and yang and the Chinese five elements, whilst the third chapter provides the basic elements of Chinese philosophy and thinking. The fourth chapter gives an introduction to the oriental approach to health and healing, which gives a further understanding of the concepts discussed in the second and third chapters. This will allow the reader to understand the Chinese way of thinking which will provide a sound grounding from which to study further. The fifth chapter gives clear and detailed instruction on how to use the *I Ching* as a divinatory tool with full examples and discussion of the potential problems which may be encountered when trying to divine with the *Book of Changes*. This should mean that you will understand and be able to use the *I Ching* without having to spend years studying the rudiments of Chinese philosophy from complicated textbooks. I have, in effect, endeavoured to place in the first part of this book all the pieces of knowledge I was lacking when I first encountered the *I Ching* and that prevented me from using it as an effective tool for divination.

The second part provides abridged meanings to the 64 hexagrams and the individual lines that make up each hexagram. It is impossible in a volume of this size to provide full details of the vast commentaries that exist regarding the hexagrams of the *I Ching*. I have, however, endeavoured to distil the essence of each hexagram and explain it in such a way as to be accessible to any reader regardless of prior knowledge or experience. As you discover the *I Ching*, you will almost certainly want to read and learn more. Many of the more academic commentaries about the *I Ching* assume that the reader has a good grounding in the philosophy and imagery of the Chinese. This can often be a stumbling block for students, but the first part of this book seeks to remedy this problem. If you choose to study further, you will be able to do so with a good understanding of the wisdom each hexagram is trying to convey. This will enable you to have access to many of the more academic studies that are now available.

Teach Yourself I Ching is designed for the general reader and serious student alike. It provides an accessible insight into ways of thinking that are alien to many Westerners but which can provide new perspectives and hence solutions to many of life's problems. The true solution to any problem is to be found only within the person experiencing that problem, but the *I Ching* provides accurate signposts that can direct your mind and thoughts towards locating that solution within you. The *I Ching* will not make you a better person, but studying its wisdom and assimilating it into your daily life will undoubtedly improve your level of health, happiness and fulfilment. You have the power to change every negative to positive, and the *I Ching* is a powerful ally and tool in the process of self-improvement. It is the destiny of every human being, if they choose to embrace it, to better themselves, to learn more and then to show others wisdom by example. If you are actively seeking truth, then this is the book for you.

One of the more interesting aspects to writing this book is that I have discovered that as I have been writing about each hexagram, I have found myself experiencing the very situation it has been describing. I even had someone telephone me and ask me the significance of the number 39 at the precise moment when I was writing about hexagram 39. The number kept coming into that person's mind and when I described the wisdom of the thirty-ninth hexagram, it answered many of the questions to which the caller had been seeking answers. This is part of the magic of the *I Ching*. It is a book of infinite complexity and infinite simplicity. It works at many different levels in many wonderful ways. The more I learn about the *I Ching*, the more I understand about myself and my place within the universal cosmos. I trust that this book may provide you with the same illumination and inspire and empower you to change negative to positive and to embrace happiness, health and fulfilment.

Part One
BACKGROUND

Chronology of Chinese History

STONE AGE (circa 600,000 BCE–circa 2000 BCE)

    Palaeolithic period (circa 600,000 BCE–circa 7000 BCE)

    Neolithic period (circa 7000 BCE–circa 2000 BCE)

HSIA DYNASTY 2205–1766 BCE

SHANG DYNASTY 1766–1122 BCE (1 Chinese Bronze Age)

CHOU DYNASTY 1122–221 BCE (2 Chinese Bronze Age)

    Western Chou 1122–771 BCE

    Eastern Chou 771–256 BCE

        Spring and Autumn period 722–481 BCE

        Warring States period 403–221 BCE

CH'IN DYNASTY 221–206 BCE

HAN DYNASTY 206 BCE–221 Common Era (AD)

    Western Han 206 BCE–9 CE

    Eastern Han 25–220 CE

THREE KINGDOMS PERIOD 221–265

CHIN DYNASTY 265–420

NORTH-SOUTH DYNASTIES 420–589

SUI DYNASTY 589–618

T'ANG DYNASTY 618–907

FIVE DYNASTIES 907–960

SUNG DYNASTY 960–1278

YUAN DYNASTY 1278–1368

MING DYNASTY 1368–1644

CH'ING DYNASTY 1644–1911

REPUBLIC OF CHINA 1911–present (since 1949 limited to Taiwan)

PEOPLE'S REPUBLIC OF CHINA 1949–present

1 | THE HISTORY OF DIVINATION IN CHINA

The history of divination in China goes back as far as writing and probably beyond. Indeed, the earliest examples of Chinese writing are inscriptions on bones and tortoise shells dating back to the last three centuries of the Shang dynasty. These inscriptions were details of divinations. Diviners of that time 'read' the cracks that appeared on shells and bones (usually the belly shell of a tortoise or the shoulder blade of an ox) that were burnt with a stick or a hot poker. After the divination was made, a record of it was inscribed on the shell or bone and it was housed in the royal archives. Thousands of such pieces have been discovered in China.

The inscriptions record many and varied divinations made on subjects as diverse as war, hunting, journeys, births, deaths, dreams, weather, the coming week or even the next few hours. Indeed, it appears that all of the important decisions of state were made only after the diviner's art had been sought. The manner and skill of reading the bones has long since been lost.

Yarrow divination is first mentioned in literature in the Classic of Documents, which is thought to have been written in the Western Chou period. Forty-nine yarrow stalks were divided up randomly into two piles and then each pile was counted through in fours with any remaining stalks being discarded. The piles were joined and again divided with the whole process repeated twice more until there were exactly six, seven, eight or nine groups of four stalks each remaining. These numbers were then used to construct a hexagram, which had specific meanings. This method was rather lengthy and a simpler method using coins instead of yarrow stalks was devised during the T'ang and Sung Dynasties. It is this method that is most used today.

The history of the *I Ching*

No one knows neither when exactly the *I Ching* was written nor whether it was the work of a single author or a particular school of tradition. Its roots go back thousands of years to a time when the sages of ancient China began to try to find ways of describing and understanding the universe. If they could understand the underlying patterns that exist in the universe, then they could begin to predict how those patterns would evolve and hence could begin to crudely predict the future, a skill which humankind has sought since birth.

The sages began to perceive the world about them as an ever-changing flow of energies. The seasons, the weather, their own growth all seemed to follow a pattern that they regarded as the products of two, primordial forces: yin and yang. There were many ways of describing these forces – here are a few: yin is passive, weak, dark and female; yang is active, strong, light and male. I should state clearly at this point that weakness and passiveness are not considered to be negative character traits, but are words used to describe transient states of being.

These two forces were written thus:

——   — —

Yang   Yin

These two forces were divided to form four new forces of yin/yin, yin/yang, yang/yin and yang/yang, which were associated with the four cardinal directions (Figure 1.1).

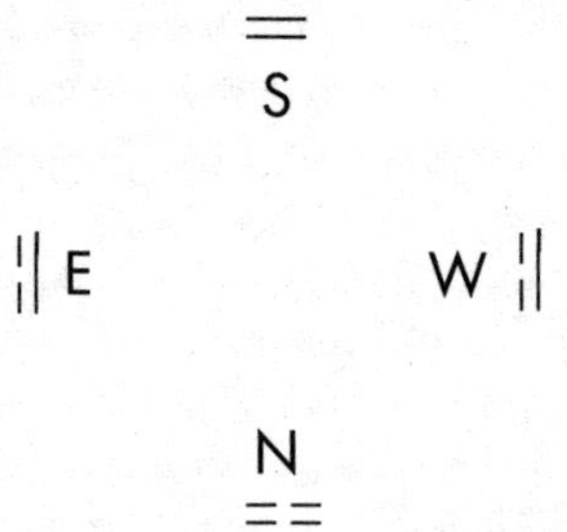

Figure 1.1   The four cardinal directions

These four forces were again divided to form eight trigrams, which were called *pa kua* and were linked to the forces of nature: Heaven and Earth, Fire and Water, Thunder and Wind, Mountain and Lake (Figure 1.2).

≡ ☷ ☲ ☵ ☳ ☴ ☶ ☱

Heaven   Earth   Fire   Water   Thunder   Wind   Mountain   Lake

*Please note that all signs in the *I Ching* are read from bottom to top or, if arranged in a circle, from the centre outwards.

Figure 1.2   The Pa Kua

Each trigram has a name and several symbolic meanings. The trigrams are said to have been discovered by the legendary Emperor Fu Hsi (twenty-fourth century BCE) written on the back of a tortoise. These trigrams were arranged in pairs to form the 64 hexagrams that make up the *I Ching*. The hexagrams are attributed to a sage named Wen-wang (twelfth century BCE), who was the father of Wu-wang, the founder of the Chou dynasty.

Wen-wang was the ruler of Chou, a state on the western frontier of China. By 1144 BCE he ruled the West of China and was posing a serious threat to the Shang dynasty. That year he was captured and imprisoned for three years by the Shang ruler. It was whilst he was in prison that he is said to have written the original *I Ching*. On his release he devoted the rest of his life to that of a sage, speaking out for peace and against the cruelty and corruption of the time. After his death, his son, Wu-wang waged war with and overthrew the Shang dynasty and founded the Chou dynasty.

During the Chou dynasty, the *I Ching* was used by the court wizards as a divinatory system. At the end of the Chou dynasty, during what is known as the Warring States period, a series of commentaries was added to the original text. During the Han dynasty (206 BCE–221 CE), the followers of Confucius (551–479 BCE) attributed some of the commentaries to their master and so the *I Ching* became one of the Five Classics (Wu Ching) of Confucianism. During this time the *I Ching* was mainly used as a divinatory system alone but in the third century CE, a young scholar, Wang Pi wrote that the *I Ching* also contained within its pages the secrets that would enable man to truly understand himself. Since then it has been used, not only for divining, but also for teaching and learning the secrets of the ancient sages, the secrets to our own existence.

In 1923, a German called Richard Wilhelm translated the *I Ching* and for the first time it became widely accessible to the West. Carl Jung and Hermann Hesse both studied the *I Ching* in depth and now there are many different translations and books about the *I Ching* available. Most emphasize only the divinatory use of the *I Ching*, but it also contains much of the foundations of Chinese philosophy and a unique perspective on the workings of the universe. Some people have even claimed that the *I Ching* contains the secrets to controlling your own future. It is the oldest book of divination and its continued popularity assures it of a secure place in the future.

The eight basic trigrams

As has already been said, the eight trigrams that form the basis of the *I Ching* each have various meanings. These meanings are then used in the *I Ching* as metaphors to explain the character and meaning of the hexagrams they make. For instance, each trigram represents a family member. Heaven (☰) represents the father. Thunder (☳) represents the eldest son. If the hexagram is made up of the eldest son above the father (☳ thunder above, heaven below), then part of the image will be of the son being more powerful than his father, having gained a level of power that is greater than his father through the lessons life has given him. Indeed, the name for that hexagram is Ta Chuang/The Power of the Great. Let us now look further at the symbolism contained within each trigram.

- ■ Ch'ien/Heaven ☰ is the father. Ch'ien is creative, active, firm, without limit. It represents the head and corresponds to strength and endurance. It also represents ice and the fruit from a tree.

- ■ K'un/Earth ☷ is the mother. K'un is receptive, passive, enfolding, gentle, fertile and modest. It represents the belly and corresponds to dedication and fulfilment. It also represents the tree-trunk and a large cart or cloth which can be said to carry all things without distinction.

- ■ Tui/Lake ☱ is the youngest daughter. Tui is joyous, inviting, and tender without but having a hard core. It represents the mouth and lips and corresponds to sensuality and pleasure. It also represents mist and the sorceress.

- ■ Li/Fire ☲ is the middle daughter. Li is clinging, bright, hollow, dry and clear. It represents the eyes and corresponds to beauty and intelligence. It also represents lightning and the sun.

- ■ Sun/Wind ☴ is the eldest daughter. Sun is gentle, flexible yet tough. It represents the thighs and corresponds to progress, perseverance and justice. It also represents wood and its characteristic of flexibility yet toughness is particularly comparable to the willow tree which features so much in Chinese literature and art.

- ■ Kên/Mountain ☶ is the youngest son. Kên is keeping still, quiet and calm. It represents the hand and fingers whose tight grip can hold things still and corresponds to a door or opening and to withdrawal and meditation. It also corresponds to the hermit who has, in Chinese tradition, always been a mountain dweller.

- ■ K'an/Water ☵ is the middle son. K'an is abysmal and fearless, that which penetrates. It represents the ear and corresponds to erosion, desire and difficulty. It also corresponds to rain and the moon.

- ■ Chên/Thunder ☳ is the eldest son. Chên is arousing and violent. It represents the foot and corresponds to determination, energy and spontaneity. It also corresponds to earthquakes and volcanoes.

As you can see, the images are very strong and evocative. When two trigrams are combined, the images help to create a picture of what the hexagram is about. The full version of the *I Ching* begins with a judgement as to the core meaning of each hexagram, which is then followed by a description of the image to further amplify the meaning. People have in the past had difficulty understanding where the images have come from and this stems from a lack of understanding of the eight trigrams that make up the *pa kua*.

The correspondences given above are by no means an exhaustive list. The trigrams have many other correspondences and a whole book could be written just about the pa kua. To exemplify this we will look briefly at one other set of correspondences, those relating the trigrams to Chinese 'internal' martial arts. The most famous of these is Tai Chi Chuan or shadow boxing although another less well-known art is actually called Pa Kua. Tai Chi is said to have been invented by Chang San-feng during the Sung dynasty (960–1278) based on his study of the *I Ching* and the movements of animals in the wild. In Tai Chi the practitioner performs a series of complex movements called a 'form'. The first part of the form is executed towards the four cardinal points of north (K'un), east (Li), south (Ch'ien) and west (K'an) with the second section of movements being executed diagonally – toward the north-east (Chên), south-west (Sun), south-east (Tui) and north-west (Kên).

Furthermore, there are eight basic movements within the Tai Chi form that are as follows: ward-off, roll-back, press, push, pull-down, split, elbow and shoulder strike. Each movement is related to Ch'ien, K'un, K'an, Li, Sun, Chên, Tui and Kên respectively. The Tai Chi form can be likened to an enactment of the *I Ching* showing the interactions that occur between the trigrams (Figure 1.3). From this one can begin to see how the yin/yang theory and its development reaches into every corner of Chinese spiritual practice from eating to exercise, meditation to how one lives one's life and so on.

Figure 1.3   The Pa Kua and Tai Chi

The hexagram and its construction

The construction of the individual hexagrams is more complex than just the joining of two trigrams. Each line has significance in both its quality (yin or yang) and its position. Before looking deeper at the line structure of the hexagram, let us first consider the two trigrams. The *I Ching* is a book that describes nature and the workings of the universe through symbols and images. Each trigram has its own image and symbolism. When two trigrams are joined, a new image is formed and with that a whole new symbology. For example, if the hexagram has Earth below and Heaven above, everything is in its proper place as it is in the world. Therefore, the symbology is one of balance. However, should the positions be reversed with Earth above Heaven, this is opposite to the natural order of the world and therefore the symbology is one of imbalance, disharmony and weakness (Figure 1.4).

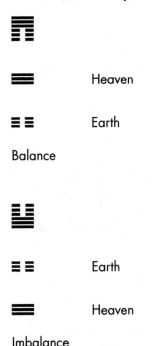

Heaven

Earth

Balance

Earth

Heaven

Imbalance

Figure 1.4   Balance and imbalance

The upper and lower trigrams can also be looked at in terms of the development of a particular event or phenomenon. The lower trigram represents the foundation or basic nature of a particular phenomenon and the upper trigram represents the consequences or development of the event. A good example would be throwing a stone into a pool of water. As the stone hits the water, ripples emanate from the point of contact outwards. If we were to represent this in a hexagram, the lower trigram would describe the action of throwing the stone and it hitting the water, the upper trigram would describe the ripples.

Each line of a trigram has significance. The position of each line is called a Yao (pronounced 'Jow' as in 'cow'). The bottom line is called the Lower Yao, the second line is called the Middle Yao and the top line is called the Upper Yao. The Upper Yao has the image of the sky or heaven. The Lower Yao has the image of the earth with the Middle Yao representing humanity that exists between the two. These are called the three powers (Figure 1.5).

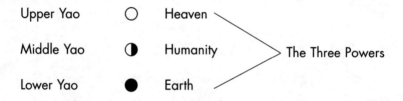

Figure 1.5   The three powers

Likewise, each line of a hexagram has significance and is referred to as a Yao. The pattern is the same as for a trigram except that each of the three powers has two Yaos instead of one (Figure 1.6).

Each of the six lines has a general characteristic which means that all first lines of all the hexagrams have similar significance, likewise all second, third, fourth, fifth and top lines.

> ■ The **first or bottom line** is associated with the early stages of development. It is symbolic of low social position, smallness, and an animal's tail.

> ■ The **second line** is the place of the subject. It is the core of the lower trigram and hence is often symbolic of being inside something subjective.

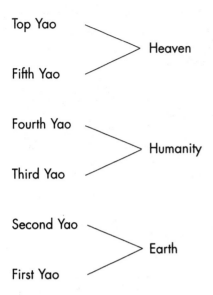

Figure 1.6   The six Yaos

- ■ The **third line** is often the line describing dangers and difficulties and is symbolic of someone trying to rise above their station without heeding the dangers, of attempting to make the hazardous crossing from the lower to the upper trigram.

- ■ The **fourth line** is the place of the officer, someone in a position of power but not in overall control – the lowest line of the upper trigram. It is usually a positive line as it shows someone who has successfully elevated him or herself from the lower to the upper trigram. It is often symbolic of a resolution to the challenges encountered in line three.

- ■ The **fifth line** is the place of the ruler, the middle (balanced/objective) place within the upper trigram. It usually symbolizes good fortune and, sometimes, supreme good fortune.

■ The **top line** is above the ruler and is often symbolic of overstepping the mark or reaching too high. Being the final line of the hexagram it can also be symbolic of an ending of one thing or situation and the birth of something new.

With all these different images, it is no wonder that people have found the *I Ching* difficult to grasp. Many men have spent many years studying it and trying to understand it further. The authors of the *I Ching* have made life much easier for us by generally commenting on the one or two images that they judge to be most appropriate to the underlying trend. This is how they have written the text, but one can see why sages have devoted years of study looking at many different images, not just those chosen by the original authors.

The sequence of the *I Ching*

Finally, we need to look at the sequence of the hexagrams. The pattern of the sequence tells the story of a man who rises from poverty, weakness and obscurity to a position of great power and renown. It is said to be loosely based on the life of the lord of Zhou, a minor chief of a western tribe who rose to become king of all China. It starts with hexagram 1 Ch'ien/The Creative representing the emergence of the protagonist. Over the following hexagrams he suffers trials and tribulations, makes a fool of himself, bides his time, raises an army and leads them through a long conflict which ends at 49 Ko/Revolution where he overthrows the king and establishes his own kingdom in the next hexagram 50 Ting/The Cauldron. Hexagram 51 Chên/The Arousing through to the end 64 Wei Chi/Before Completion describes the rise of a new pretender to the throne as he makes his own advance.

There are many other patterns that emerge throughout the *I Ching* – opposites, reflections between hexagrams and so on – but these patterns will emerge of their own accord as the *I Ching* is worked with.

2 | THE ORIGINS OF YIN AND YANG

The ancient Chinese philosophers called the time before the world was created Wu-Chi, which means ultimate nothingness. This is slightly misleading when translated into English because how can something come out of nothing? A better paraphrase would be chaos. Wu-Chi was a state of disorganized formlessness, which is about as close as our finite minds can get to describe it. It is like trying to view something through a steamed-up window – you know the object has form but you cannot make it out, it is a hazy image of confused vagueness. As you clear the window, you can begin to perceive the form more clearly, you can tell where it begins and ends, you can tell its shade and colour and that of the background. You are beginning to perceive yin and yang.

Chinese creation theory states that out of Wu-Chi was born Tai Chi and from this came yin and yang. The Tai Chi symbol is now very well known but its true meaning is less well known. Many people think it is just the sign of the martial art of the same name but it is much more than that. It is the symbol that describes the creation of the universe, the innermost workings of that universe and it is a pictorial representation of the dynamic interaction of yin and yang (Figure 2.1).

Figure 2.1   The yin/yang symbol

What are yin and yang?

When a room is empty, it can be likened to the state of Wu-Chi. As soon as people enter the room, the state of Tai Chi begins. The people interact, some are dynamic and extrovert whereas others are quieter and more introvert. The differences between people can be described in terms of yin and yang. Extrovert people are more yang and introvert people are more yin. In general, the characteristics of yang are male, hot and moving. The characteristics of yin are female, cold and still. Yin and yang appear to describe opposites. Day is yang and night is yin. The sky is yang and the earth is yin and so on. Most people do not have any problem understanding this concept. The problems occur when they ask a question such as 'Is a cold man running on the earth during the day yin or yang?' The answer is both, as I will now explain.

Yin and yang are not absolutes but transient states of being. Water boiling in a saucepan provides an excellent example. The water at the bottom of the pan, nearest the heat source is hottest and rises (yang) and this allows the slightly cooler water at the top to fall (yin) where it is heated and rises (yang). Although the water is boiling, it is in a constant state of flux and therefore exhibits both yin and yang qualities, as do all things in the universe. Absolute yin and yang do not exist. Everything in the universe is forever changing, nothing is truly still, and the only constant is change.

Yin and yang do not exist unless there is someone there to perceive them. If one fills three bowls with cold, warm and hot water respectively and then places the left hand in the hot water and the right hand in the cold water, the left hand feels hot (yang) and the right hand cold (yin). If after 30 seconds both hands are placed in the bowl of warm water, to the left hand the water feels cool (more yin) and to the right hand the water feels warmer (more yang). So the question arises 'Is the bowl of warm water yin or yang?' Again the answer is both and totally dependent upon the point from which you perceive the bowl. Comparing the cold water and the warm water, the cold water is yin and the warm water is yang. Comparing the warm water and the hot water, the warm water is now yin and the hot water is yang. Finally, comparing the hot, cold and warm water, the hot water is yang, the cold water is yin and the warm water is the balance between the two. You see, it all depends upon the point from which you perceive the phenomenon.

Yin and yang are ways of comparing one set of characteristics. Going back to our original question of the cold man running on the earth during the day, one can describe each of the aspects as yin or yang but one cannot compare non-related aspects such as coldness and maleness. One can only describe them in terms of yin and yang separately.

George Ohsawa, the founder of modern-day Macrobiotics, in his book *Zen Macrobiotics* gives 12 theorems about yin and yang called The Twelve Theorems Of The Unique Principle. Macrobiotics is best described as a way of living according to the principles of yin and yang. This, on a simple level, means that practitioners eat foods that keep them in balance with their environment, i.e. in a hot (yang) climate, more cooling (yin) foods are eaten and vice versa. On a deeper level, it is aiming to live every moment of every day in balance and harmony with everything. Let us now look closely at these 12 theorems:

1 **Yin and yang are the two poles of the infinite pure expansion.**

   This means that the whole universe ('the infinite pure expansion') can be described in terms of two opposite and complementary forces – yin and yang.

2 **Yin and yang are produced infinitely, continuously, and forever from the infinite pure expansion itself.**

   This means that the universe goes on forever and that anything that manifests out of that universe can be described in terms of yin and yang.

3 **Yin is centrifugal; yang is centripetal.**

   This means that yin things produce expansion, lightness, coolness, and that yang things produce compaction, weight and heat. In terms of foods, fruit with its juiciness and cooling nature is considered yin, and root vegetables with their compactness and warming nature are considered yang.

4 **Yin attracts yang; yang attracts yin.**

   This is usually where people become confused and say things like 'That means that if I think good thoughts, then I'll attract bad things to me, which doesn't make sense'. They are forgetting that you can look only at one thing at a time in terms of yin and yang. They are trying to compare good and thoughts with bad and actions. How it works is that thoughts are yin and actions are yang; so good, positive thoughts will attract good, positive actions. This then agrees with that old saying 'What you sow (yin), you will reap (yang)'.

5 **All things and phenomena are composed of yin and yang in different proportions.**

This means that nothing exists that cannot be described in terms of yin and yang jointly. With regards to our original experiment with the bowls of water, the hot bowl can be described as being most yang (and therefore least yin), the warm water can be described as having yin and yang in balance, and the cold water can be described as most yin (least yang).

6 **All things and phenomena are constantly changing their yin and yang components. Everything is restless.**

Nothing is static. A chair that appears still and solid is actually made up of millions of moving atoms and it rests on a spinning planet that is circling the sun in a spinning galaxy. Everything is always changing and therefore the yin and yang components in everything must be forever changing.

7 **There is nothing completely yin or completely yang. All is relative.**

Returning once more to our experiment, the hot (more yang) water can always be made hotter (even more yang) and therefore must always have a yin component.

8 **There is nothing neuter. There is always yin or yang in excess.**

Because everything is changing, perfect balance between yin and yang can never exist. Things that appear balanced are in a state of dynamic (moving) equilibrium.

9 **Affinity or force of attraction between things is proportional to the difference of yin and yang in them.**

Everything is proportional; so the more good, positive thinking you do, the more good, positive actions you will attract. And, of course, the reverse is also true.

10 **Yin expels yin; yang expels yang. Expulsion or attraction between two things yin or yang is in inverse proportion to the difference of their yin or yang force.**

Opposites attract, like repels is well known even in Western society from both social and scientific circles and it stands to reason that the more opposite two things are, the more they will attract.

11 **Yin produces yang; yang produces yin.**
    Thoughts lead to actions, which in turn lead to more thoughts.

12 **Everything is yang at its centre and yin at its periphery (surface).**
    This naturally follows on from the third theorem.

You can see that although yin and yang are simple, they are also infinitely complex. If you want to see this in action then I can suggest nothing better than looking at Fractal Geometry and the Mandelbrot Set which is one of the most extraordinary discoveries of modern science. Fractal Geometry is the study of simple, mathematical formulae requiring no more than addition and multiplication, which produce 'pictures' that are of infinite complexity and infinite size. Arthur C. Clarke, the writer of the film *2001: A Space Odyssey*, explains it simply in his video, *Colours of Infinity*.

The five elements

Out of the theory of yin and yang came the theory of Wu-Hsing. Wu-Hsing is usually translated as the five elements, powers or breaths. Wu means five and Hsing means walks or moves which implies a dynamic process and these five elements are used to describe and differentiate between different phenomena. The five elements are water, fire, wood, metal and earth. It should be said that the Chinese do not believe that all matter is made up of these five elements in a literal sense, rather that these elements possess different characteristics which can be seen in all matter and phenomena. For instance, the element water does not refer to the substance, but rather to the properties of the substance soaking and descending (water always flows down). Fire is hot and moves upwards (like flames rising), metal is pliable and can be melted, moulded and then hardened. Earth nourishes and wood represents growth.

The Chinese noted that everything ran in cycles (seasons, growth, the moon, etc.) and they used the five elements to describe this cyclic nature. They called this the *principle of mutual creation*: wood creates fire, fire creates earth, earth creates metal, metal creates water and water, in turn, creates wood (Figure 2.2). The image of wood creating fire is one of rubbing two sticks together to make fire. The fire then produces ash, which becomes part of the soil. Compaction in the earth leads to the creation of metal ores. Metal creating water is a less obvious image although this may relate to the ritual practice of leaving a metal mirror exposed to the night (perhaps in order to catch the moon's energy) and observing the formation of dew on it. Finally, trees rely on water for growth and so water was said to create wood.

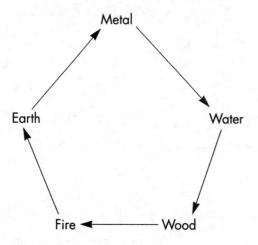

Figure 2.2   The principle of mutual creation

The same pairings were also linked in reverse order by the *principle of mutual closeness*, which meant that each element was regarded as being attracted to its source in the same manner that a child is naturally attracted to its mother. So wood is close or attracted to water, water to metal, metal to earth, earth to fire and fire to wood (Figure 2.3).

There is also a further pairing of properties called the *principle of mutual destruction* and the *principle of mutual fear*. The first principle states that each element has its 'enemy' that weakens it. The earth is weakened by wood taking nutrients out of it, wood is weakened by metal in that metal axes are used to chop down trees, metal is weakened by fire because fire melts metal, fire is weakened by water because water extinguishes fire and water is weakened by earth because earth forms natural barriers to limit the flow of water as in rivers and lakes (Figure 2.4).

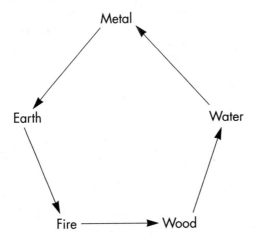

Figure 2.3   The principle of mutual closeness

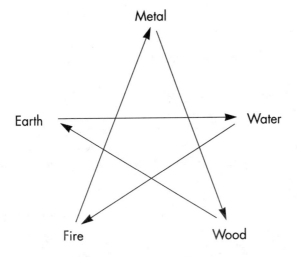

Figure 2.4   The principle of mutual destruction

Finally, the principle of mutual fear states that each element has fear or respect towards its natural predator thus: wood fears metal, metal fears fire, fire fears water, water fears earth and earth fears wood (Figure 2.5).

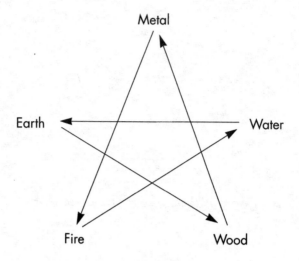

Figure 2.5   The principle of mutual fear

The yin/yang theory and that of the five elements not only provided a way of describing all natural phenomena but they also formed the basic principles behind traditional Chinese medicine from physiology and pathology to disease description, diagnosis and treatment. Table 2.1 shows some of the correspondences of the five elements relating both to natural phenomena and to medicine.

Table 2.1   Table of correspondences

Element	Wood	Fire	Earth	Metal	Water
Direction	East	South	Centre	West	North
Season	Spring	Summer	Indian summer	Autumn	Winter
Climate	Windy	Hot	Damp	Dry	Cold
Emotion	Anger	Joy	Pensive	Grief	Fear
Taste	Sour	Bitter	Sweet	Pungent	Salty
Sense organ	Eye	Tongue	Mouth	Nose	Ear
Yin organ	Liver	Heart	Spleen	Lungs	Kidney
Yang organ	Gall bladder	Small intestine	Stomach	Large intestine	Urinary bladder
Tissue	Tendons	Blood vessels	Flesh	Skin	Bones
Western element	Fire	Water	Ether?	Air	Earth

3 | FOUNDATIONS OF ORIENTAL PHILOSOPHY

Since the dawn of time, humankind has sought ways to describe the universe it lives in. In the West, we have sought to measure and quantify through science, and indeed much of modern Western thinking is based upon scientific thought. As Western science has advanced, our ways of describing the universe have become increasingly complicated and inaccessible to most people. The Chinese, on the other hand, have always sought simple ways of describing the world around them that can be understood by any individual. In this chapter, rather than look at the major figures in Chinese philosophy such as Lao Tsu and Confucius, we shall look at the basic attitude to living that the ancient Chinese created and show that it is as relevant today as it was thousands of years ago.

The ancient Chinese sought to describe every aspect of the universe in simple terms and from that came the theory of yin and yang and the Chinese five elements as described in Chapter 2. The ancient Chinese used these theories and others to understand the world about them and how to live in peace and harmony within that world. All human beings seek balance in their lives and we shall use the lessons of Chinese philosophy to learn how this can be achieved.

Personal responsibility

You are responsible for everything that happens to you. This does not mean that everything negative that happens to you is a punishment from God because you are bad. What it means is that you attract every situation to yourself in order to learn. Understanding this simple truth means that you can have power in every area of your life. You are no longer a victim of fate but a student of life. When something that you perceive as negative happens to you, you have two basic ways of dealing with it. The most common way in the West is to become resentful that fate has dealt you such a hard blow. You may even feel anger towards another individual who has wronged you and this feeling can sometimes stay with you for the rest of your life. Such feelings weaken you and allow others to have a negative influence over you. On the other hand, a Chinese sage would tell you to ask the question, 'Why have I attracted this into my life and what is it trying to teach me?' If, through honest, careful thought and self-analysis, you learn an important lesson from the situation you will have become a better, stronger and wiser individual. The idea of needing to forgive a person who has wronged you ceases to exist because they have merely helped you to become better, wiser and stronger. They have, in effect, helped you to learn. This is how to turn any negative situation into a positive one. Everything in life is significant and everything you experience you 'attract' in order to learn. The more you learn the wiser you become and the closer you get to health, happiness and fulfilment.

Westerners tend to resist change, and yet the ancient Chinese understood that the only constant in the universe is change. By learning to embrace change, we can learn how to flow with the energies of the universe. This, in turn, leads us to a fuller understanding of the process of change in the world around us and in our own lives. The *I Ching* describes this process and this is why it is called 'The Book of Changes'. Everything has a beginning, middle and end. Once we understand this, we can stop resisting change and allow it to unfold naturally while learning from it. This transforms you from a humble victim of fate into an active participant in your unfolding learning process.

The five spiritual aspects

Out of the Chinese five element theory come the five spiritual aspects. They describe different aspects of living that need to be balanced in order for us to be healthy, happy and fulfilled individuals. These aspects are called Chen, Shen, Hun, Po and I.

- **Chen** relates to the Chinese element of water. Water flows downwards and Chen has the same motion. Chen is determination and the power to get 'down' to things. It relates to physical work and groundedness.
- **Shen** relates to the Chinese element of fire. The flames of a fire have an upward movement and Shen describes a sense of upliftedness and raised spirits. It is linked to relaxation, rest and nourishment.

■ **Hun** is linked to the Chinese element of wood. A tree spreads out in every direction when it grows and so Hun relates to self-expression and destiny (i.e. the manner in which you express your life).

■ **Po** is linked to the Chinese element of metal. Metal is formed through compression. Ores in the earth are drawn together to form metals and so Po is linked to drawing in the lessons we need to learn. We learn most of our lessons through interaction with other people and thus Po also relates to our social interaction.

■ **I** is linked to the Chinese element of earth which is regarded as the centre of the universe as we perceive it and so I is the point of balance where all the other four spiritual aspects combine.

To put this in simple terms, we need to have all four aspects of Chen, Shen, Hun and Po in balanced, dynamic equilibrium if we are to be balanced individuals. We need a time to work (Chen) and a time to rest (Shen). We need a time for self-expression (Hun) and a time for social interaction (Po). Without all four aspects, the fifth aspect (I) is imbalanced. Understanding this allows you to look at your own life and to see clearly the areas where you need to find balance. The saying 'All work and no play makes Jack a dull boy' shows clearly the relationship between Chen and Shen. We understand this but so often we fail to understand its importance in terms of our happiness, health and fulfilment. It is interesting to note that there is a further link to health because each of the aspects is linked through the five elements to specific organs. For instance, Shen and the element fire relate to the heart. It is no coincidence that many workaholics suffer from heart attacks. Equally those people who do not allow themselves self-expression are often very angry which is a sure sign of liver imbalance. Hun and the element wood relate to the liver and the emotion attached to this is anger (see Table 2.1 at the end of Chapter 2).

Po is linked to the element metal and the lungs. The lungs draw in air and we learn through attracting or drawing lessons to ourselves as we saw earlier. Po can be described as being about quality and resources. We are all born with certain resources and we seek, throughout our lives, to acquire new resources (or skills) and to improve the quality of the resources we already possess. We do this mainly through social interaction. Sometimes you meet a person for the first time and feel an instant rapport with him or her. It may even seem that after only a few minutes of meeting you feel as if you have known the other person for years. This is because he or she has resources or qualities that you need and equally you have resources and qualities that the other person is seeking. As you talk and discuss matters, you are subconsciously trading qualities and resources with each other.

This trading of qualities and resources is a continually unfolding process that takes place with everyone you meet. Furthermore, due to the laws of yin and yang, the two parties in this trading process have an equal and opposite amount to trade. This means that you have as much to learn from someone as you have to teach. This may not appear to be the case, but anyone who has been involved in any form of teaching will tell you that you learn as much from those whom you teach as they do from you, the lessons are just different. Many people, especially in relationships, concentrate upon trying to teach rather than trying to learn. You can, in truth, only really teach by example. Words have no meaning without experience. Words without experience create knowledge. Words with experience create wisdom.

Relationships

The spiritual aspects relate not only to individuals but also to our relationships. You can use them to understand and assess problems in relationships. For a relationship between a couple to be balanced, it too requires the four aspects of Chen, Shen, Hun and Po in balance. If I encounter problems in a couple's relationship, I ask the following questions:

- Are you physically attracted to each other? This relates to the aspect of Chen because Chen is about the physical (e.g. work) and about groundedness (the sexual union between man and woman is perhaps one of the most grounding actions).

- Do you love each other? This relates to Shen with its sense of nourishment and upliftedness.

- Do you have qualities and resources to share (i.e. do you have things to learn from each other and are you willing to learn them)? This, as we have already seen, relates to Po.

- Are your lives heading in the same direction? This relates to Hun and how you express your lives.

In most cases, there are one or more areas where there is not balance and by highlighting these areas and working to restore them to balance, the problems can be solved if both parties are willing to work on their areas of imbalance.

This is the beauty of the Chinese approach to living. Everything is inter-related and you can use these ideas to view any aspect of life. Health problems such as heart disease, liver imbalance, asthma, etc. can all be linked to the five elements and the spiritual aspects. For instance, people with heart problems need to improve their Shen. People with liver imbalance need to learn better expression of their emotions and destiny and so on. Understanding the interconnectedness of all things enables you to find balance and harmony, which in turn leads to happiness, health and fulfilment.

All aspects of Chinese philosophy teach us this power of balancing our own lives. In the West lives are ever more complicated, so full that Westerners fail to see the significance of many of the things attracted into their lives. Western diets are full of complex chemicals and additives that feed the senses rather than stimulating the mind. Perhaps Westerners can learn from the simplicity of the Oriental way of thinking. Simple does not mean stupid. It means understanding the way in which the universe operates and aligning our energies to that way. This is what the Chinese word 'Tao' means, *the way*. In Chinese philosophy there is no Christian way, Hindu way or Buddhist way, there is just *the way*. This philosophy is not dependent upon any religious belief, but on a simple understanding of the infinitely complex universe. By learning *the way*, you will learn about life itself.

Dependency

Once you begin to understand the five elements and the five spiritual aspects, you will see more and more ways in which they can be applied to life and its problems. In the West many issues surround dependency and these too can be viewed in terms of the five spiritual aspects. As with all things there is a yin and a yang aspect to dependency, a positive and a negative side. Let us first look at the four types of negative dependency.

1 **Our physical, emotional and spiritual nourishment**.
   This type of dependency is linked to the Shen aspect. We are dependent upon all sorts of things that rob us of our power

and energy. If you look to other people to lift your spirits and to make you feel happy, you are giving your power away to those people. If you rely upon substances such as tea, coffee, sweets, cakes, cigarettes, alcohol or drugs to lift your spirits, then you are giving your power away to those substances. Your happiness should not be dependent upon anything or anyone. If your happiness depends upon the people you care about being nice to you, you are allowing them to control your emotions. If your happiness is not complete without certain foods, drinks or drugs, then you are allowing those substances to weaken you.

The only person you can depend upon for your happiness is yourself. True happiness can be found only by looking within your self. All the time you seek happiness through external stimuli, you will be forever disappointed. Happiness comes from learning to heal yourself of all your pain and trauma. Many people say that they would be happy if their external circumstances changed (for example, if they had more money or time) but this is an illusion. To be happy you must learn acceptance. You must learn to accept where you are and seek your happiness within your present circumstances. Any problem that you have, is only a problem because of how you perceive it. If you can learn to change your perspective, you will find solutions instead of problems. True happiness comes when you can eat a plain bowl of rice with the same amount of pleasure that you would eat a banquet. Happiness can be found in any situation, even in pain and suffering through learning acceptance.

2 **Co-dependency or feeding others' wants**.
The easiest example is the person who buys an alcoholic a bottle of whisky. They are feeding the problem and compounding the other person's dependency. This relates to the spiritual aspect of Po – the sharing of negative resources. We all have a tendency towards co-dependence because we often spend our time trying to make other people happy at the expense of our own happiness. If you seek to make others happy at the expense of your own happiness, you will be showing by your example only how other people can do

the same. If you really love and care about another person, the best thing you can do for them is to seek your own happiness. Once you have found your own happiness, you can then teach them how to find their own happiness. This is much more beneficial to both parties than trying to please each other. Many of us are born 'pleasers' living unhappy lives of self-sacrifice.

3 Dominance or independence.

This relates to Chen and often manifests as selfishness. There are many people who are pleasers outside of their own homes and selfish, dominant individuals at home. Dominant people tend to seek out dependent people and they can give the impression of being very happy and satisfied with their selfish, unfeeling attitude to life. They are lying to themselves and those around them. The path to true happiness can never be found through such behaviour.

4 Non-dependency.

These are individuals who are self-absorbed and tend not to interact with others. They don't play the dependency game and may tell you that they are truly free, but their lack of communion with other people starves them of their opportunities to learn and to express themselves. This relates to Hun and this type of behaviour leads to emotional stagnation and inner frustration.

The fifth aspect, **I**, can be likened to interdependence, the positive side of all these aspects. The positive side to dependence is knowing when to ask for help. The positive side to co-dependence is knowing how and when to give help. The positive side to dominance is having the ability to hold on to your power and determination when others try to rob you of it, and the positive side of non-dependence is knowing when to get out of a situation for your own safety and well being. True interdependence means that you can always be flexible and adapt to life's changing situations with ease, thus maintaining your inner calm and happiness. This is the true power of interdependence.

This leads us to study one further question – what does it mean to give help to others. So often we regard this as using our energies to make someone else's life easier but is this always being kind? Imagine that you are visiting friends who have a young child. When you arrive at their house, the mother has lit a candle in the room you are talking in. The child goes up to the candle and is about to touch the flame. The mother, seeing this, stops the child and warns it of the dangers of fire. A little later, when the mother's attention is not on the child, you notice it going up to the flame again. What is the kindest or most helpful thing to do? Most people's immediate answer would be to stop the child, but is this really the best thing? Suppose you do not tell the child anything but allow it to burn its finger. This may give the child a very unpleasant experience, but one that will teach it the valuable lesson of respect for fire. This, in turn, may save its life countless times. Suppose on the other hand that you decide to warn the child and as a result the mother blows out the candle. The child has lost the opportunity to learn that lesson. What if the very next day the child learns the lesson instead by pulling a kettle full of boiling water over itself and suffering severe burns? Which action is the kindest? From this example it is clearly much better that the child learns respect for fire from a minor burn on the hand than a major burn all over its body.

You can see from this example that the decisions we make out of a desire to help other people may not always be the most helpful decisions. You must judge carefully how you help other people. It is sometimes better to allow a person to make a mistake and learn from it, than to deny him or her the opportunity to learn by warning of what you perceive as that person's ill-chosen actions. Remember that it is through personal experience that we learn the most. The person who makes no mistakes in life, dies an old fool. The person who makes lots of mistakes in life, but learns from each and every one becomes the wisest of the wise.

Healing from the past

Oriental philosophy states that the past is just a memory, the future just a dream. Here and now is the only place that you can truly have an effect. Many of us tend to live with regret about the past, unable to heal from the traumatic experiences that we have had. It has already been said that you attract everything that comes into your life in order to learn. Does this really mean that if you have been abused, raped or otherwise traumatized that you attracted it? The answer is yes, but remember that is has nothing to do with sin or punishment. It has to do with learning.

Many people have suffered some form of abuse in their lives. Often they are so hurt by their experience that it stays with them for life. This means that the 'sick' individual who perpetrated the act is continuing to have a negative influence on that person's life. If, on the other hand, they can learn to heal from that trauma and find release from their deep pain, they will be able to apply that learning to all pain in their lives. This will then turn the negative experience into a positive one and allow them to be truly free from pain. In life we often need to experience the negative side of things to find the positive side.

To experience light, you must experience darkness. To find peace, you must first experience turmoil. The wonderful thing is that, according to the laws of the universe, if you are in pain, you can experience and equal and opposite amount of joy. If you search within yourself you can turn anger to love, sadness to happiness, tears to laughter and dependence to freedom. Yin turns to yang and yang turns to yin. If you can find true happiness, health and fulfilment, it will make all of the negative things that you have experienced worth it. Our ultimate goal should be to learn so much from the past, to find so much peace and happiness in our lives, that we can say 'I would not change any of the past because of where it has led me to in the present'. Without learning to heal from the past, we have no future.

4 FOUNDATIONS OF ORIENTAL MEDICINE

Understanding Oriental medicine can give valuable insights into the *I Ching* and the Chinese concepts of health, healing and energy. Chinese medicine is amongst the most ancient medical systems used in the world today. Its foundations go back to the same source as the *I Ching* and with the development of the *I Ching* came the development of Chinese medicine. Ancient does not mean primitive and, indeed, the Chinese medical system is one that allows for the effective treatment of *all* known diseases.

In the West, a doctor asks the question, 'What symptoms is this patient suffering from?' He or she looks at the symptoms and tries to eradicate those symptoms with surgery and/or drugs. If the illness does not respond to either therapy, then it is usually regarded as 'incurable'. The Chinese doctor asks the question, 'What kind of patient is manifesting these symptoms?' He or she looks to understand the underlying imbalance within the patient and treat that rather than concentrating upon the symptoms. Fortunately, the Chinese understand how to re-establish balance which, in turn, means that any illness is potentially curable.

Early Chinese medical research was performed upon living subjects whereas Western medical research was performed largely through the dissection of dead bodies. This is why the Chinese have a concept of energy and its role in healing whereas Western doctors tend to view the body purely as a machine (because dead bodies have no energy). By looking at the body as a machine, Western doctors see outside pathogens attacking that machine in the form of bacteria and viruses and they seek to eradicate those pathogens. The problem is that such micro-organisms evolve at a frightening rate so that no sooner has one illness been eradicated, than another new variety of illness comes to the fore.

The Chinese view things in the opposite way. They understand that a healthy individual has a natural ability to ward off infection so they seek to make every patient into a healthy individual. This may seem simplistic but Western science is beginning to understand this approach. It is now known that most bacteria, fungi and viruses cannot thrive in an oxygen-rich environment. If a patient has good levels of oxygenation throughout his or her body, it is impossible for these pathogens to get a hold.

One further difference between the Western and Oriental approach to healing is that in the orient, all illness is regarded as your body's way of communicating to you that something is not right. Once you understand what your body is trying to communicate to you, there is no need for the illness to manifest in your life. This attitude can actually be applied to all of life. If there is any situation in your life that you find unpleasant, once you have learnt everything that that situation has to teach you, it will cease to manifest in your life. Fighting the situation or illness will only give it energy to feed from. By accepting the situation and learning from it, you draw energy away from the situation until it has no energy left to exist.

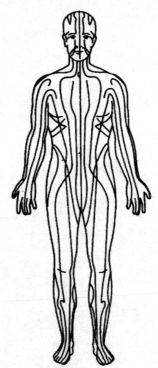

Figure 4.1 The meridians

Chi and the meridians

The Chinese have long understood that underlying imbalance within an individual manifests as energy imbalances. This energy, or *Chi* as it is called in China, flows throughout the body in *meridians* or pathways (Figure 4.1). There are 14 major meridians with 12 of them relating to the function and balance of the 12 major organs. These 12 organs are divided into yin and yang and are called *Zhang-Fus* where *Zhang* refers to the yin organs and *Fu* refers to the yang organs. The six Zhang organs are the lungs, heart, spleen, kidneys, liver and pericardium. The six Fu organs are the large intestine (or colon), the small intestine, the stomach, the urinary bladder, the gall bladder and an organ called *San Yao* or the 'Triple Heater' for which we have no Western equivalent. The other two meridians run along the front midline of the body and the back midline through the spine.

Each major organ in the Chinese medical system has a flow of energy that rises and falls over the course of a day. If an organ is weak, it is treated at the time when its energy is highest and if an organ is overworking it is treated at the time when its energy is lowest. The highest and lowest energy patterns of each organ is as follows:

Meridian name	Highest energy flow	Lowest energy flow
Lungs	3–5 a.m.	3–5 p.m.
Large intestine	5–7 a.m.	5–7 p.m.
Stomach	7–9 a.m.	7–9 p.m.
Spleen	9–11 a.m.	9–11 p.m.
Heart	11 a.m.–1 p.m.	11 p.m.–1 a.m.
Small intestine	1–3 p.m.	1–3 a.m.
Urinary bladder	3–5 p.m.	3–5 a.m.
Kidneys	5–7 p.m.	5–7 a.m.
Pericardium	7–9 p.m.	7–9 a.m.
Triple Heater	9–11 p.m.	9–11 a.m.
Gall bladder	11 p.m.–1 a.m.	11 a.m.–1 p.m.
Liver	1–3 a.m.	1–3 p.m.

NB: All times give in GMT.

This ebb and flow of energy is another example of the dynamic interaction between yin and yang. Even the energy of the body can be viewed in terms of yin and yang. The energy flowing through the body's organs and meridians is called *Yang Chi* and can be regarded as more yang than the energy that flows through the skin and muscles which is called *Wei Chi*. Wei Chi is described as 'defensive energy' and some Chinese martial art masters develop so much Wei Chi that they can have bricks and heavy paving slabs broken upon their heads and chests without causing them any harm. One of the most famous techniques to build up Wei Chi is called 'Iron Shirt Chi Kung'. Practitioners can develop their skills to such a level that two masters can have the point of a double-pointed spear pressed against each of their throats and then walk towards each other placing such tension upon the spear that it snaps in two. They use nothing to protect the sensitive area of their throats except Wei Chi. Such superhuman acts can occasionally be witnessed at Chi Kung exhibitions in China.

The actions of the major organs

The Chinese have a completely different model that they use to describe the body and the functions of the main organs. The heart, for instance, is regarded as much more than the pump that powers the blood around the body. It also has control over the blood vessels throughout the body and is strongly linked to the mind and emotions. Depression and sadness are symptoms of heart imbalance as are most circulatory disorders. The heart is the most important of all the major organs and is protected by the pericardium.

The liver is regarded as storing the blood and maintaining free flow of energy around the body. It governs the free expression of emotion, the free flow of bile and stops stagnation of the blood and other bodily fluids. It is also linked to the eyes and controls the muscles and tendons. This means that eye problems, muscle strain, stress, blood clots and emotional suppression are all liver related and can be treated successfully by improving the balance and energy flow to and from the liver.

The spleen in Chinese actually refers to the spleen and pancreas and is the organ that handles digestion. It controls transportation and transformation within the body. It also keeps the blood in the vessels, nourishes the muscles (giving them their shape), keeps the body upright and holds the internal organs in place. This means that nose bleeds, excessive bruising, prolapse and poor muscle tone are all regarded as symptoms of spleen weakness.

The lungs control Chi and the breathing. They disperse the energy we get from breathing to the skin (in the form of Wei Chi) and descend fluids to the kidneys. They also control the skin and hair. This means that asthma, eczema and poor hair are all regarded as symptoms of lung imbalance.

The kidneys control all the body fluids and separate the pure from the impure. They hold our energy down (keeping us grounded) and control the brain and the nervous system. They are also connected to the ears. This means that nervous disorders, epilepsy and ear problems are all regarded as signs of kidney imbalance.

The eight principles

Chinese medicine has eight principles or stages of illness that are divided into four pairs with each pair being linked to yin and yang. The eight principles are as follows:

1 External (yin)
2 Internal (yang)
3 Hot (yang)
4 Cold (yin)
5 Excess (yin)
6 Deficiency (yang)
7 Collapse of Yin (yang)
8 Collapse of Yang (yin)

Collapse of Yin is regarded as a yang condition because yang is in dominance just as Collapse of Yang is regarded as a yin condition because yin is in dominance. The scale of 1 to 8 is one of increasing severity where 1 is the least severe and 8 is close to death.

External conditions manifest in the Wei Chi (i.e. the skin and muscles) whereas internal conditions manifest in the Yang Chi (i.e. the organs and meridians). Hot conditions the body to overwork whereas cold conditions slow the body down. Excess conditions can be one of eight possibilities:

1 **Energy (Chi)** – One can never have too much Chi but one can have stagnant Chi where there is an excess of energy within one particular area of the body.

2 **Blood** – Likewise one can never have too much blood within the body. This again refers to a condition of stagnation where there is a build up of excessive blood in one area.

3 **Cold** – This is a more severe version of principle No.4 (Cold) where there is an excessive amount of cold in one or more areas of the body.

4 **Heat** – This is a more severe version of principle No.3 (Heat) where there is an excessive amount of heat in one or more areas of the body.

5 **Wind** – This is always in excess but has nothing to do with flatulence (which is stagnant Chi). It refers to the wind that blows around us. The energy of the wind can get inside the body. Sneezing is one of the ways we release excess wind that has invaded the body. It is also the factor that explains why some pains move round the body. There is a type of arthritis that is caused by wind invading the body. Sufferers experience extreme arthritic pains that move around the body. One day it can be in a hand, the next in a hip, next the ankle, then back to the hand and so on. The symptoms can be so severe that the affected area can be rendered useless while the attack lasts. Western doctors tend to treat patients suffering from this very real and painful illness as a psychiatric problem and often tell patients that it is impossible for pain to move around the body in this way so it must be 'all in the mind'. This is a mistake that renders the illness incurable to Western doctors. Acupuncture is very effective at eliminating excess wind from the body and so can successfully treat this condition.

6 **Damp** – This usually manifests as an excess of unprocessed fluids as in water retention or oedema. Swollen ankles are often a damp condition.

7 **Phlegm** – This refers to excess mucous anywhere within the body. Excess phlegm causes stagnation that, in turn, is one of the principal causes of cancer.

8 **Food** – This can either be in excess (overeating) or in excess due to stagnation (e,g, sluggish digestion and/or constipation).

Deficient conditions can be one of four possibilities:

1 **Energy** – Either an overall deficiency within the body or a deficiency in one or more organs.

2 **Blood** – Either an overall deficiency within the body or a deficiency in one or more organs.

3 **Body warmth** (yang) – This is never in excess, only deficient. A fever is regarded as an excess of heat, not an excess of body warmth.

4 **Body fluids** (yin) – This is never in excess, only deficient (e.g. mild dehydration).

Collapse of Yin is caused by a combination of extreme heat with a deficiency of body fluids leading to severe dehydration (e.g. in a desert). Collapse of Yang is caused by a combination of extreme cold with a deficiency of body warmth leading to severe hypothermia (e.g. at the North Pole).

One can also get combinations of the eight principles as follows:

- ■ **Deficiency of Yang** – This occurs when there is a full amount of body fluids but not enough warmth (a combination of cold and deficiency).
- ■ **Excess of Yang** – This occurs when there is a full amount of body fluids but too much heat (a combination of heat and excess).
- ■ **Deficiency of Yin** – This occurs when there is a full amount of body warmth but not enough body fluids (a combination of heat and deficiency).
- ■ **Excess of Yin** – This occurs when there is a full amount of body warmth but external cold (a combination of cold and excess).

N.B. Remember that there can never be an excess of body warmth or body fluids.

The causes of disease

There are three categories of causes of disease, external, internal and miscellaneous.

External

External refers to weather conditions and is divided into sub-categories:

- ■ **Cold** – This causes contraction, stagnation and pain (e.g. cold causing muscles to become shorter and stiffer).

- **Wind** – This causes mobile pain especially in the upper part of the body.
- **Heat** – This causes redness and sweating.
- **Dryness** – This is like heat but with a deficiency of body fluids.
- **Fire** – This is an extreme version of heat and manifests as inflammation.

It is worth noting that some external characteristics can be caused internally, for example eating cold food can cause cold to invade the spleen.

The common cold is regarded as cold and wind invading the lungs. A clear, running nose is the body expelling cold. The wind takes the cold into the body via the lungs and the skin (which is linked to the lungs). If, on a cold winter's day you breathe through an open mouth rather than through your nose, you are likely to be invaded by cold. If it is windy as well, you will need to keep mobile to stop the wind from invading you. If, on a cold windy way, you are attending a football match, it is better to be playing than spectating. The players keep mobile and warm whereas the spectators tend to be relatively immobile and cold.

When a person with a cold starts to produce yellow phlegm from the nose and chest, this is the body expelling heat from the lungs. The cold condition has become a hot condition. This is a bit like a car engine on a frosty morning. If an engine is frozen and you manage to get is started, the cold will stop the oil from circulating efficiently leading to friction, which in turn leads to heat. It is also the same with inflamed joints. Cold gets into the joints first and stops the free flow of synovial fluid in the joint.

Friction then causes the joint to become inflamed. An acupuncturist would usually use heat in the form of a burning herb called 'moxa' (mugwort) on the far end of an acupuncture needle that has been inserted in the afflicted area. This may sound strange, to use heat to treat a hot and inflamed joint, but the root of the problem is stagnation (lack of flow of blood and synovial fluid) caused by coldness. By heating the area internally, the circulation is stimulated and the inflammation is drained away by the body's own blood flow.

The best way to combat these external causes is to build up good Wei Chi through Tai Chi or Chi Kung (Chinese energy building exercises).

Internal

These are emotional causes and perhaps the most important group because the Chinese believe that all illness begins in the mind. There are seven major emotions as follows:

■ **Fear** – This is irrational fear and is linked with the kidneys. The kidneys keep us grounded and so fear is a sign of kidney weakness. One of the more extreme manifestations of this emotion is the 'panic attack'. If you witness someone having a panic attack, you will see that his or her energy is rising upwards. The face becomes red and often sweaty, the shoulders hunch up and the breathing becomes restricted. This is because the kidneys have not been strong enough to ground this fear-filled energy.

■ **Anger** – This relates to the liver and is linked to a lack of free flow of energy and self-expression. If we become angry with someone, it is usually a sign of our own internal imbalance. Other people's words make us angry only if there is some truth in them that we do not wish to face. Anger at other people's actions is sometimes self-anger at our inability to stop those actions or to foresee them.

■ **Depression** – This is linked to the heart and is a lack of inner joy. This is usually because we are not being true to our spiritual path and ourselves. People who suffer from depression have usually given their power away to other people, situations or addictions (including food and drugs). Examples of this include allowing others to bully you into doing things you do not really want to do or looking for external change or additions to bring internal happiness. True happiness comes from within and is not dependent upon anything or anyone.

■ **Fright** – This is different from fear and is related to the pericardium and heart. It refers to any shock or 'fright-full' situation.

■ **Anxiety** – This is linked to the lungs and relates to a lack of understanding of the order of the universe and the laws of yin and yang. Once you understand how energy works and interacts, you will cease to have anxieties.

■ **Grief** – This too relates to the lungs and refers to grief that is held onto. It is perfectly normal to grieve for the loss of a loved one. If, however, you are still consumed with grief a year later, this is not healthy and will cause physical illness.

■ **Worry** – This is different from anxiety. Worry is thinking round and round in circles. It is linked to the spleen and is also often linked to unhealthy eating.

We can look at these emotions in terms of the five spiritual aspects that we discussed in Chapter 3. Fear is a lack of control and power and is related to weak Chen. People with good Chen tend to do well in fearful situations. Soldiers, for example, are trained to build up high levels of Chen. If you are crossing a road and a car comes towards you, how you react is dependent upon your level of Chen. If you have poor Chen you are likely to freeze with fear and be hit by the car. If you have good Chen you are likely to have the presence of mind to run and do your utmost to avoid being hit.

Anger is related to Hun and is a trigger to help you to get your life back on track. Anger is a symptom of lack of expression and if held on to can cause serious illness such as cancer. Holding on to anger and then letting it out explosively leads to injury, either of yourself or those around you.

Depression can be viewed as a lack of Shen. Part of the answer is to actively seek those things that lift your spirits and make you feel good. It is important though to be wise about how you choose to lift your spirits. Taking sugar or drugs to create a false euphoria will not solve the problem nearly as efficiently as a walk in the park or spending time with friends who have good Shen.

Anxiety in linked to Po because it is caused by a lack of resources to deal with the tasks that face us in our lives. The answer is to find those resources. In its simplest form, if you are anxious about your driving test because you are not very good at reversing, the answer is to keep practising reversing until you *are* good at it. Then you will cease to be anxious.

Grief is the body's process of slowly re-establishing lost resources and is also linked to Po. This is because those we love are resources in our lives; i.e. they are people we learn a lot from. Grief is a way of adjusting to not having that potential for learning from a particular individual. We miss all the things that they brought into our lives and grief is a way of finding new or different resources to fill that gap.

Worry is linked to I, the fifth spiritual aspect and is usually due to the poor quality of the other four aspects.

All held-on-to negative emotions are caused by biochemical imbalance and the chief cause of this imbalance is the first category of the miscellaneous section, food. If you eat a proper, balanced diet you should ultimately find freedom from all such emotions.

Miscellaneous

Miscellaneous covers several diverse areas as follows:

■ Food – You are what you eat. Mother nature has provided a sensible guide to balanced eating by providing seasonal foods in every climate of the world that are balanced for the people living in that climate. Macrobiotics is the study if yin and yang as it relates to food and it has the following guidelines:

1 Eat in harmony with the season where you are living.

2 Eat in harmony with the climate where you are living.

3 Eat mainly whole grains and vegetables (preferably locally grown).

4 Chew every mouthful of food 50 times or more.

5 Drink only when thirsty and only as much as it takes to quench the thirst.

6 Word hard physically if you are well.

7 Cook using traditional methods (i.e. using a naked flame and steel, cast iron or terracotta cooking pots).

8 Avoid excessive animal products especially if you live in or are going to visit a warm climate.

9 Avoid vinegars and all industrial foods (i.e. those with additives, preservatives, colourings or artificial flavourings).

10 Your diet should include 60 to 70 per cent grains and 20 to 25 per cent well-cooked or baked vegetables.

11 If you have a yin illness (most Western illnesses are yin caused by over-consumption of yin foods) avoid all chemicals, potatoes, tomatoes, peppers, eggplant and fruit.

Both cold and wet food and weather adversely affect the spleen and hence the digestion. The Chinese recommend that food should be eaten regularly, warm and it should be clean (i.e. free from bacteria as dealing with bacteria takes a lot of Chi). Much of the obesity in the Western world is caused by the over-consumption of cold foods leading to an accumulation of phlegm within the body. Food should make us feel good during *and* after a meal and should be prepared and eaten in an atmosphere of love and peace.

■ **Physical** – This covers physical injuries and depletion of life-force (called Jing by the Chinese). Jing can be depleted in women by bearing too many children and by men through ejaculating too much. The *Classic of the Simple Girl* written during the Sui Dynasty 589–618 CE gives the following guidelines as to the maximum healthy level of frequency of ejaculation for men:

Age	In good health	In average health
15	2 times a day	Once a day
20	2 times a day	Once a day
30	Once a day	Every other day
40	Every 3 days	Every 4 days
50	Every 5 days	Every 10 days
60	Every 10 days	Every 20 days
70	Every 30 days	None

■ **Exercise** – The best exercise is one that you will not have to give up as you get older. Tai Chi, Chi Kung and Yoga are all especially good for all ages and levels of fitness.

■ **Trauma** – This relates to violent injuries e.g. stabbing, car crash, etc.

■ **Parasites, plagues and pollution** – This includes intestinal worms, disease-carrying animals and pesticides in the food chain.

■ **Geopathic stress** – This mainly relates to low-level EMF's (electro-magnetic frequencies) emitted by pylons, electrical equipment, mobile phones and microwaves.

- **Phlegm** – This causes all manner of ailments including cysts, boils, respiratory problems and cancer.
- **Blood** – When stagnant this can cause tumours, period pains and cancer.
- **Stress** – Perhaps one of the biggest causes of ill health in the modern world.

This overview of Chinese medicine shows clearly again the interconnectedness of the oriental worldview. To the Chinese, everything is significant and often seemingly unrelated ailments can point to a common cause. How you live, eat and think all has an effect upon your health and well-being. The West could learn much from studying the Eastern approach to life and living. Remember that every action has a reaction that can reverberate through many lives. Understanding this means that you are careful how you think and act. This is fundamental to oriental thinking. Even today, most Chinese and Japanese businesses (including some well-known electronics companies) consult the *I Ching* before making any major decisions so that the health of the business and all the individuals employed by that business is kept at an optimum level through remaining in harmony with the universe. They understand that consulting the *I Ching* can help one to remain in harmony with the path of one's destiny, which is the path to happiness, health and fulfilment.

5 | USING THE *I CHING*

How to cast

I have found that the best way to get to know the *I Ching* is to start using it as soon as possible. You have a lifetime in which to discover the finer points of Chinese philosophy, but the *I Ching* can start guiding and teaching you immediately. Using the oracle requires no special knowledge or skills. An open mind and a desire to learn are all that are needed.

There are two main methods of casting the *I Ching*. One is with yarrow stalks and the other, much simpler, method is with three coins. I have only ever used coins but have always found this method produces perfect results.

You will need the following:

- a pen and paper
- three coins of the same size and denomination
- a question or situation that you want commenting on.

The question/situation can be anything from 'Should I take this new job offer?' to 'What is my life all about at present?'. Hold the coins in either hand and just think about the question/situation for a few minutes. You are now ready to cast.

Building the hexagram

Most coins have a head and a tail side with the head side showing the portrait of one of the country's leading monarchs or heads of state. Chinese coins often have one side with many Chinese letters on it (this side is taken as heads) and one side that is blank or has fewer letters on it (this side is taken as tails). You are going to throw the coins all together and add up the total scored. Heads count as three, tails as two. There are four possibilities as follows:

3 heads (scores 3+3+3) = 9
2 heads + 1 tail (scores 3+3+2) = 8
1 head + 2 tails (scores 3+2+2) = 7
3 tails (scores 2+2+2) = 6.

Repeat this procedure five times so that you end up with six totals, for example:

1st throw – 1 head + 2 tails	scores 7
2nd throw – 1 head + 2 tails	scores 7
3rd throw – 3 tails	scores 6
4th throw – 2 heads + 1 tail	scores 8
5th throw – 3 heads	scores 9
6th throw – 1 head + 2 tails	scores 7

So in this example the scores are 7,7,6,8,9,7.

The first throw represents the first line of the hexagram, which is the bottom line. The second throw represents the next line up and so on with the sixth throw representing the top line. Each total represents a different type of line as follows:

Total 6 = a broken line changing to a solid line
Total 7 = a solid line
Total 8 = a broken line
Total 9 = a solid line changing to a broken line.

So our example hexagram would look like this:

Sixth line total	7	
Fifth line total	9	
Fourth line total	8	
Third line total	6	
Second line total	7	
First line total	7	

If your totals are all 7s and 8s then you have what is called a single hexagram. If, however, you have one or more 6s or 9s in your totals then you have what is called a changing hexagram.

Single and changing hexagrams

A single hexagram means that the answer to your question is very clear and you read the meaning only for that hexagram (i.e. not the section entitled 'The lines'). A changing hexagram means that the answer is more complex and you form a second hexagram by changing the lines containing six or nine. In our earlier example the two hexagrams would be as follows:

1st hexagram

2nd hexagram

As you can see, changing any lines whose total is 6 or 9 creates the second hexagram.

The lines

With a changing hexagram you look up the first hexagram and read the meaning. Then you continue to the next section entitled 'The lines'. You then read the extra interpretations corresponding to the changing lines, for example in our example we have a 6 in the third line and a 9 in the fifth line. These interpretations generally tend to comment on the things that have led up to the question/situation or to give a suggested course of action. You then look up the second hexagram and read the meaning only. This part usually refers to the possible outcome of a situation or contains the final clarifying answer to your question.

How to interpret

Each hexagram (set of six lines) is made up of two trigrams (sets of three lines), a lower trigram (the first three lines from the bottom up) and an upper trigram (the top three lines). In our example, the lower trigram of our first hexagram is ☱ (Tui) and the upper trigram is ☴ (Sun).

If you refer to the key at the back of the book, you will find the number of your hexagram(s) and can then look it (them) up in the interpretation section.

Before reading the interpretations, clear your mind of any preconceived ideas and then carefully read each part of the interpretation. Spend a short while meditating on what each section is saying and on how it relates to your question. Then proceed to the next section if there is one (i.e. if you have a changing hexagram). At the end of this you should have an answer. If you are still unclear on what the *I Ching* is saying, put the reading to one side and come back to it later when your mind is in a different state.

If, after doing this, you are still unclear, rephrase the question or ask another question related to the same issue and re-cast the coins. This should then provide further clarity. Finally, if you are still unclear it means that this is not the right time for you to find the answer. There are things ahead of you that need to come to pass before the answer will become clear. Have patience.

In our example, we would look up and read the following:

1st hexagram is 61 Chung Fu. We would read the introduction and meaning plus the meanings for 6 in the third place and 9 in the fifth place.

2nd hexagram is 26 Ta Ch'u. We would read the introduction and meaning only.

Here are some examples from real life:

Example 1

Alison came to me wanting to know what to do next in her life. She had met a man with whom she hoped to move to the country but, as they had got to know each other, it had become clear that although they could remain friends, sharing a home together would not be right at the moment. Alison had found a property and wanted to know whether she should move there on her own or not. She cast the coins and produced the following result: 7,7,7,8,9,9. With two 9s in her scores she had a changing hexagram as follows:

	1st hexagram	2nd hexagram
9	——O——	—— ——
9	——O——	—— ——
8	—— ——	—— ——
7	————	————
7	————	————
7	————	————

The first hexagram was 9 Hsiao Ch'u (☴). The first line of the meaning spoke loud and clear 'The time for action has not yet come'. It said that she still had work to do on herself and obstacles to overcome. Reading the lines produced further clarity. Nine in the fifth place said, 'Loyalty will lead to strong bonds between friends' referring to the fact that she needs to maintain her friendship with the man she had met despite the fact that their initial plans together had not worked out. Nine at the top further confirmed that this is not the time to advance. The second hexagram was 11 T'ai (☷) and the short, sweet meaning was 'A time of peace and harmony is at hand. Good fortune and success abound. It is as if heaven is on earth.' From this I was able to tell her that if she continued to work on herself and her own things, remained friends with her man and did not move yet, that the outcome would be wonderful and her dream of a house in the country would come true. At the time of writing, Alison was sorting all sorts of things out in her life, was really positive and was looking forward to the fulfilment of her dream when the time was right. Because she knew the future was good, she was happy to embrace the process of self-change knowing that it would lead to a positive outcome and, incidentally, the bond of friendship between her and the man she met has grown stronger and sweeter.

Example 2

John had decided that it was time to change career. His current job was not providing him with satisfaction and there were limited career prospects. John wanted to know whether to leave his job before he had secured another position or whether to stay while actively seeking a new career. He had few financial commitments and so could afford to be out of work for several months. He consulted the *I Ching* and threw the coins with the following result: 9,7,8,8,8,7. With one 9 in his score he had the following changing hexagram, 41 Sun/Decrease with 9 at the beginning changing to 4 Mêng/Youthful Folly.

	1st hexagram	2nd hexagram
7	─────	─────
8	── ──	── ──
8	── ──	── ──
8	── ──	── ──
7	─────	─────
9	──●──	── ──

The hexagram Sun spoke of the need for balance and for simplifying his life. It said that restriction would bring clarity and John certainly felt his job was restrictive. The 9 at the beginning talked about learning and sharing wisdom which John found encouraging as he was planning to seek a new career in teaching. The hexagram Mêng spoke very clearly about the need to learn more and fully understand each lesson before proceeding on to the next one. It also spoke about the need for him to seek out a teacher and to thoroughly master his subject. John had been wondering about going back to college and the *I Ching* seemed to confirm that. He remained in his job until he found the right college course and has since successfully retrained and is now working as a teacher.

Example 3

Peter had been very successful in business but felt that he had no real friends, only acquaintances. He felt as if it was time to change his life but did not quite know how. He consulted the *I Ching* asking it to comment upon the situation. He threw the following result: 7,8,7,7,8,6. This gave rise to the changing hexagram 55 Fêng/Abundance (Fullness) with 6 at the top becoming 30 Li/The Clinging, Fire.

	1st hexagram	2nd hexagram
6	—— X ——	————
8	— —	— —
7	————	————
7	————	————
8	— —	— —
7	————	————

Fêng spoke to Peter very much about how he was feeling. Life was good but he felt the decline through lack of friendship. The line 6 at the top really hit home as Peter had been very ruthless and arrogant in his business dealings and he realized that this attitude had pervaded all areas of his life and was the reason why he was lacking friends. At first he was downhearted by this reading but Li offered him a solution. It talked about aligning to the earth and searching out truth and enlightenment. Shortly after this reading he went along to a workshop by a Native American which included a sweatlodge which is a purification and healing ceremony. There Peter experienced an honesty and openness that he had never experienced before that changed his whole perspective on life. The last time I spoke to him he was actively involved in various workshops and groups and had found an inner peace and friendships that he never believed possible. He certainly experienced first hand the power and magic of the *I Ching* to initiate positive change.

What to do when answers are unclear

Occasionally when you consult the *I Ching*, the answer makes limited or no sense. There are two main reasons for this. The first is that you have asked a poor or too general question (e.g. 'Will I be successful?'). The solution to this is to rephrase the question and recast the coins (e.g. 'How can I find success in my life?'). The other reason is that you are asking questions which should not be answered at this time. This is because sometimes knowing the answer to a question will unduly influence you and therefore deprive you of the opportunity to learn important lessons. This becomes apparent when you rephrase the question and still get a confusing answer. The solution to this problem is to accept that it is not the right time to know the answer, to let it go and concentrate on learning the lessons that are manifesting into your life right now.

Finally, it must be said that the *I Ching* is a serious book and needs to be approached with respect. It is not a source of party games and will not provide you with entertainment. If approached with respect and an honest desire to learn, the *I Ching* will give you great wisdom and increase your understanding, but ultimately it cannot initiate change in your life, only you have the power to do that.

Nuclear hexagrams

Imagine that you are stuck in a traffic jam. You look out of your window and you can see some cars ahead and some behind. Consulting the *I Ching* is like viewing the traffic jam from the air above. It will not get you out of the jam, but it will show you clearly how you got there and the most efficient way to get out of it. Most of the time when we consult the *I Ching*, we are concerned only with how to get out of a situation. If you would like to know why you are in a given situation, you need to construct a nuclear hexagram. Nuclear, as its name suggests, gives you the heart of the problem. For example, if you have just lost your job and would like to know the best way to get another one, consult the I Ching as normal. If, on the other hand, you would like to know why you lost your job, through your coins as usual with this question in mind, form a nuclear hexagram and look up its meaning only. This will give you an insight into the past. This technique is little known in the West but is well practised in the East.

How to make a nuclear hexagram

Once you have thrown the coins and formed your initial hexagram, take the second, third and fourth lines as the first, second and third lines of your nuclear hexagram; then take the third, fourth and fifth lines as the fourth, fifth and sixth lines of your nuclear hexagram. If, for example, your initial hexagram was

then the 2nd, 3rd and 4th lines are ☳

and the 3rd, 4th and 5th lines are ☵

so the nuclear hexagram is ䷜.

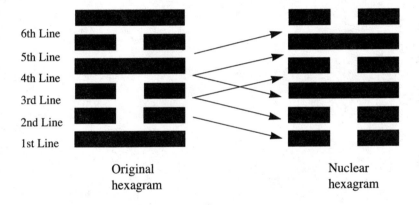

Original   Nuclear
hexagram   hexagram

Part Two
THE HEXAGRAMS

6 THE 64 HEXAGRAMS OF THE *I CHING*

1 Ch'ien/The Creative

Above Ch'ien   The Creative, Heaven
Below Ch'ien   The Creative, Heaven

The first hexagram is composed of six unbroken lines. These represent the primal unstoppable strength of the creative. There are no weak lines and so strength endures the test of time and remains unchanged. In human terms it denotes the creative principle within humanity whose inspiration comes from the higher, spiritual self.

The meaning

If you continue on your path, seeking always what is right and true, success is assured. If you draw this hexagram, success comes from the primal depths of the universe and is dependent upon you seeking a path of happiness. This is the path of your destiny because the path of happiness and destiny are one and the same. By seeking that which makes you truly happy, you will naturally be seeking your spiritual path. It is only through perseverance that success will come. Perseverance here means remaining true to oneself, standing firm in one's beliefs. Standing firm does not mean standing still, for you must always strive to better yourself, embracing lessons as they come and remaining determined to continue on a spiritual path even when the going gets tough. Trust that everything that comes to you, good or bad, is coming to teach you lessons that are the stepping stones to the realization of your dreams.

The image

There are two heavens in this hexagram and yet in reality there is only one heaven. Two heavens give the image of movement, the enduring nature of heaven through time. This image teaches that for you to have durability on your spiritual path, you must be consciously striving to get better and stronger by recognizing and working on your weaknesses rather than trying to hide from them.

The lines

Nine at the beginning means:

There is a right time for everything and timing is of the essence here. If you wait patiently and calmly, not trying to force issues, the right time to act will appear but has not yet come. Watch, wait and remain true.

Nine in the second place means:

It is time to walk your talk. This will ultimately lead to you having great influence on others just by remaining true to yourself. One can change others only by changing oneself. Lead by example.

Nine in the third place means:

As you become successful, you attract more attention from others and your fame spreads. This is good providing you do not allow the adulation of others to take you off your path. Ambition must not be allowed to compromise integrity. Remain true and be wary of the dangers of success.

Nine in the fourth place means:

A very clear choice presents itself here. You can soar to great heights and have an important role to play in society, or you can withdraw from the world and, through solitude, can further develop yourself. Remain true to yourself and the right decision will become apparent. Remember whatever decision you make will be right. The only wrong thing to do is to make no decision.

Nine in the fifth place means:

'Birds of feather flock together'. By seeking and attracting like-minded people, many opportunities for mutual learning will manifest.

Nine at the top means:

Do not become so engrossed with your spiritual path that you lose touch with the rest of humankind. This will inevitably lead to failure. Do not bite off more than you can chew and remain humble.

When all the lines are nines it means:

Act gently but remain strong in your decisions and good fortune will come.

2 K'un/The Receptive ⚏⚏

Above K'un   **The Receptive, Earth**
Below K'un   **The Receptive, Earth**

The second hexagram is composed of six broken lines. It represents the primal, earthly, receptive power of the feminine and is complementary to the first hexagram. Complementary does not mean opposite, it means working with rather than against. The physical should always be led by the spiritual, this is why heaven is represented by strong lines and earth by weak lines. If the physical becomes too strong, to the detriment of the spiritual, then imbalance and disharmony can be the only result. Equally, to attain true spiritual heights, one needs to be well grounded. Heaven and earth are equally important just as the spiritual is expressed through the physical body in thoughts, words and deeds.

The meaning

You must allow yourself to be guided on your path. Now is not the time to lead for this would only lead to you losing your way, now is the time to be led. There are things to be done, but you will need help and guidance from others for success to be assured. This does not mean that one puts responsibility on others and sits back and watches. On the contrary, perseverance and hard work are called for on your part. There will be a time to work alone and a time to seek the assistance of others. Follow your intuition and success will be yours.

The image

The two heavens in the first hexagram represented the duration of time. Here, the doubling of the earth represents space in terms of the earth being a vessel that can carry all things that dwell upon it. The earth bears all, good and evil. So too must you learn to develop a character of breadth and purity so that you can help and support all that you meet upon your path.

The lines

Six at the beginning means:

Winter is approaching and so a time of consolidation is nigh. You are entering a dark phase in your life that can bring you much wisdom. Look within and learn from the past so that when the spring arrives, you will not have to re-learn old lessons.

Six in the second place means:

Nature does not judge, it just is. Align yourself to nature and you will find yourself becoming more harmonious and balanced. As does nature, let your actions speak for themselves.

Six in the third place means:

Do not allow pride and vanity to come upon you. Whether you work alone or in the service of others, exercise restraint. Do not seek the adulation of others. Be satisfied with working to the best of your abilities, remain humble and your actions will bear much fruit.

Six in the fourth place means:

Wherever you are, alone or in the public eye, you must maintain reserve. Allowing yourself to become too well known at this time will only make you a target for others. Seek neither blame nor praise.

Six in the fifth place means:

When working in a position of prominence, but not independent of others, great discretion is called for if success is to be assured. It is not a good time to make those around you aware of your talents as it may create jealousy.

Six at the top means:

Do not seek confrontations, in such situations there can be no winners, only losers.

When all lines are sixes it means:

In this situation the hexagram of the Receptive changes into that of the Creative. This means it is best to stand firm. Stand by your truth and all will be well.

3 Chun/Difficulty at the Beginning ䷂

Above K'an   The Abysmal, Water
Below Chên   The Arousing, Thunder

This hexagram can be likened to a blade of grass pushing against an obstacle as it struggles to find its way out of the earth and into the light. This is why it is called 'difficulty at the beginning'. Although this is symbolic of hardship and tests, one knows that just as the blade of grass eventually finds its way to the light, so the difficulties will not last for ever. Everything has a beginning, middle and an end. Storms bring thunder and rain, but after the storm there is freshness in the air and a release of tension.

The meaning

This is a time of great potential growth. It is almost like a birth into a new understanding, but before that understanding can be realized, there is a time of chaos and great difficulties. Out of chaos comes order and the reward for overcoming these difficulties will be great. This is not a time to stand alone. Seek help from others and tread the path with caution. There are many dangers ahead but perseverance will reap its own rewards.

The image

Out of chaos comes order. It is like having a ball of wool that is full of knots. Once you have untangled it, you can use it to create something beautiful. To find your true place on the path, you must be able to stand alone or united with others.

The lines

Nine at the beginning means:

When you encounter an obstacle at the beginning of an endeavour, it is unwise to try to force yourself through it. Take a moment to pause and think. To make progress you may need to humbly seek the help of others. Remember that without humility you will not attract the help you need. Do not allow this obstacle to deter you from your goal.

Six in the second place means:

The road is beset with obstacles and difficulties. Suddenly help appears from an unexpected quarter. Be careful! There are almost certainly conditions to the help that will ultimately hinder you on your path. It is best to ride out the storm alone and politely refuse the help. Be patient, things will become calmer and all will turn out well in the end.

Six in the third place means:

Seek guidance before making decisions. Rash actions and seeking the easy way out will lead only to failure. You are in unfamiliar territory and need to seek a guide.

Six in the fourth place means:

You are in a situation where you need to act, but lack the power to do so. An opportunity to connect with the right helpful energies must be seized with neither pride nor reserve. If the right help is found, all will go well.

Nine in the fifth place means:

Tread the path one step at a time and good fortune will be yours. Trying to force the issue or proceeding too quickly will end in disaster. Quietly and faithfully tread the path and gradually the road will become easier and obstacles will disappear.

Six at the top means:

The initial difficulties have proved too great for a successful outcome to be possible. It is time to abandon things and seek new paths. If you do not heed this, there is a danger that you will get bogged down and lose sight of the path completely.

4 Mêng/Youthful Folly ䷃

Above Kên   Keeping Still, Mountain
Below K'an   The Abysmal, Water

Water springs from the foot of the mountain not knowing where fate will take it. This image represents the inexperience of youth. Folly should not be thought of as stupidity, but merely a lack of experience. Remember, there is also a carefree daring about youthfulness that can sometimes speed the path to success.

The meaning

You need to recognize the areas of your life where you lack experience and seek out a teacher who can help you to gain more knowledge in these areas. The emphasis here is on you seeking a teacher, not waiting for one to find you. When you have found a teacher, you must make sure that you ask pertinent questions and do not waste their time with trivialities. Seek knowledge with great sincerity and master each lesson before seeking to proceed further.

The image

The image here is of a spring flowing from the foot of a mountain. It does not stagnate because, as it flows, it fills up every crevice and hollow and thus flows onward. So it must be with your learning. Do not skip lessons but determine to thoroughly master your subject.

Six at the beginning means:

Self-discipline is called for. Lessons must be taken seriously if progress is to be made, but do not let discipline become a restrictive drill for this will only lead to humiliation.

Nine in the second place means:

Do not let your inner strength dominate your outward dealings with others. Suffer fools (i.e. those with less experience than yourself) with grace, for you may learn much. Listen to the feminine within and success will come.

Six in the third place means:

Do not give your power away to those who are stronger than you. Do not worship those you admire. Such actions will bring no good. Instead, bide your time and learn from others until you have the strength and knowledge to hold your own with them.

Six in the fourth place means:

Do not allow yourself to become entangled in wild and unrealistic fantasies for they will lead only to humiliation. In such situations, a teacher's only recourse is to abandon the student and allow him or her to learn from his or her own mistakes.

Six in the fifth place means:

Seek instruction with child-like humility. Being devoid of arrogance will allow you to learn a great deal and assure you of good fortune.

Nine at the top means:

Sometimes an inexperienced person oversteps the boundary of what is acceptable and needs pulling up, but this should be done with graciousness and with the intent of preventing further harm, not causing more.

5 Hsü/Waiting (Nourishment) ䷄

Above K'an   The Abysmal, Water
Below Ch'ien   The Creative, Heaven

The rains nourish the land but come in their own time. In the same way we, who seek spiritual nourishment, must be patient and wait for it to come.

There is also the image of strength facing danger. In such a situation, the strong person bides his or her time rather than plunging forwards or running away.

The meaning

You are faced with danger that must be overcome. This will not be achieved through impatience or weakness. You must look within to seek the answer, but you will find it only if you look with open eyes unclouded by self-delusion. When the answer comes, action must be swift and resolute. Furthermore, fate comes when she wills. At times of peace one should not worry about the future, but should live in the present while nourishing spirit, mind and body.

The image

When the clouds gather, one can but wait for the rain. It is the same with your path. The future will unfold in its own time; so be patient, seek to remain balanced and do not try to interfere with things before it is the right time.

The lines

Nine at the beginning means:

The danger is not yet at hand. Life appears to be normal, yet there is a sense of something impending. The key here is to carry on life as normal as possible for as long as possible. In this way you will be able to face the danger with full strength when it comes.

Nine in the second place means:

The danger is closing in. General unrest leads to arguments and disagreements. The person who remains calm is the one who will succeed.

Nine in the third place means:

You have shown your colours too early and have placed yourself open to attack. Take great care. This is a serious situation that requires all your attention if you are to emerge unscathed.

Six in the fourth place means:

The situation is extremely dangerous. Do nothing. Allow fate to take its course and concentrate on maintaining your composure. Action will only block your escape.

Nine in the fifth place means:

In the midst of danger come moments of peace and tranquillity. These should be used to renew one's strength. Beware of losing sight of the danger. Remain focused and good fortune will eventually come.

Six at the top means:

The waiting is over; the danger can no longer be avoided so one must yield to fate. Everything seems to have been in vain, all appears to be lost. Then, suddenly, events take the unexpected turn. This must be embraced for although at first one is unsure whether it has come to kill or to cure, it will lead to deliverance and good fortune.

6 Sung/Conflict

Above Ch'ien   The Creative, Heaven
Below K'an   The Abysmal, Water

The upper trigram has an upward movement, lower trigram a downward movement (water flowing down). The two halves are moving in opposite directions, giving rise to the idea of conflict.

The meaning

Conflict comes when you meet opposition on your path. Remain clear minded and yet be willing to overcome the opposition by meeting your opponent halfway and negotiating. This is not a time for new ventures, as they will fail if the forces behind them are not united. The only way to avoid conflict is to be watchful and wary from the very beginning. Search out areas of disharmony and resolve them before they reach the conflict stage.

The image

The image indicates that disharmony has risen to a level where conflict is inevitable. To avoid this situation one must do only what is right and always seek balance.

The lines

Six at the beginning means:

When you see conflict is coming, drop the issue. Do not try to force decisions. In this way the dispute will be minor and all will end well.

Nine in the second place means:

If your opponent is stronger, there is no disgrace in retreat. Back down before you get others around you involved in a full-scale battle.

Six in the third place means:

The only virtues that cannot be taken from you are those you have earned through merit. No one can take them away from you. Sometimes you must let your opponent appear to win to bring about peace. If you are sure of the truth within yourself, it matters not what others think.

Nine in the fourth place means:

You need to find peace within to proceed further. The lack of peace makes you inclined towards confrontation but this is not advised. Accept your fate, find your peace and good fortune will follow.

Nine in the fifth place means:

Provided you are in the right, things will go well.

Nine at the top means:

If you carry on a conflict to its bitter end and win, happiness will not be long lasting as you will find you have attracted further attacks and so the conflict will not end.

7 Shih/The Army

Above K'un   The Receptive, Earth
Below K'an   The Abysmal, Water

Water is stored in the earth like an army is 'stored' within the general populace during peacetime, but is ever ready for the moment conflict breaks out. The attributes of the hexagram are danger within, obedience without. This, again, is like the army which is potentially very dangerous but is held in check by its commander.

The meaning

War should always be a last resort. To win any battle the army must be fit and healthy in spirit, mind and body and have complete loyalty to its commander. Also the commander must make sure that the passion of war and the glory of victory do not lead to unjust acts. If the battle is fought with justice and perseverance, all will go well. So it is with a person who decides to enter any type of battle. Self-control, discipline and fitness at all levels are vital.

The image

Victory in war is dependent upon the state of mind of those fighting that war. Those who have been protected and nourished by their government during peacetime make the fiercest warriors.

The lines

Six at the beginning means:

To enter into battle, the cause must be valid and just and the army must be ordered for victory to be assured.

Nine in the second place means:

This line represents the strong warrior who is appointed to lead the army. Everyone in the army must know their place and purpose and carry out all deeds with honour.

Six in the third place means:

If those who have not been chosen as leader interfere in matters, misfortune will follow. A leader must be strong and resolute.

Six in the fourth place means:

If the opponent is too strong, the only course of action is to retreat and there is no dishonour in this.

Six in the fifth place means:

If one is attacked, combat is justified but it must be an ordered retaliation. The army must not be allowed to degenerate into a 'free for all' as this will only lead to misfortune.

Six at the top means:

The war is over and victory won. Everyone who fought is rewarded according to their station but the chain of 'command' (e.g. the mind) must remain in place so that 'inferior people' (e.g. negative emotions) do not gain places of power.

8 Pi/Holding Together (Union) ䷇

Above K'an   The Abysmal, Water
Below K'un   The Receptive, Earth

Water flows from the earth to unite with the water of the seas. The one strong line in this hexagram represents the leader who unites and binds the people together.

The meaning

You need to unite with others so that each person complements the others. For this to be successful there needs to be a leader. You need to ask yourself honestly if you have the attributes to be that leader; for such a position has great responsibility and requires a strong spirit and much wisdom. If you are not that person then you need to join a group that already has a good leader. Social interaction can lead to many lessons.

The image

The image is of water flowing together to fill the empty places of the earth. So, too, when humans come together, the community needs to flow together so that each individual member feels a part of the whole.

The lines

Six at the beginning means:

Honesty and sincerity are fundamental in the forming of good relationships. Let your inner strength speak louder than your words.

Six in the second place means:

Humility and perseverance of action will lead to good relationships with others. Arrogance will lead to failure.

Six in the third place means:

Be wary of associating with the wrong people, i.e. those people who can offer you no opportunities for growth. Do not let such people stop you from meeting and associating with those who can help you. Retain your freedom and integrity.

Six in the fourth place means:

Do not hide from others relationships that are beneficial for you. Be open about your attachments while remembering to remain constant and not be led astray.

Nine in the fifth place means:

If you are a leader, do not try to woo followers. Whoever chooses to follow, let them follow. Those who walk away should be allowed to depart in peace. This way, a leader will have only loyal followers who have made their choices of their own free will. If you choose to follow another, make sure it is your choice alone, made by your own free will.

Six at the top means:

He who hesitates is lost. If you hesitate for too long, the moment of potential union may be lost and you may realize your error too late.

9 Hsiao Ch'u/The Taming Power of the Small ䷈

Above Sun   The Gentle, Wind
Below Ch'ien   The Creative, Heaven

The wind gently holds the clouds in check so that they can become denser and eventually produce rain, but the time for rain has not yet come. The strong is being temporarily held in check by the weak. Only through gentleness can success be assured.

The meaning

The time for action has not yet come. This is not unfavourable as there is the prospect of ultimate success, but there are still obstacles to be overcome. Only through gentle persuasion can you exert any influence. You need to be strong in your resolve within yet gentle in your actions. Use this time to further work on refining yourself.

The image

The wind does not blow for ever. In this time when you can have no great effect on the outer world, use your energies to refine your inner nature.

The lines

Nine at the beginning means:

Do not try to overcome obstacles by force for you may find yourself committing to a direction from which there is no turning.

Nine in the second place means:

Although you would like to press forwards, you see from others that the way is blocked. The time is not right to press forward; so you should retreat with others of like mind rather than expose yourself to potential harm.

Nine in the third place means:

An attempt has been made to press forwards forcibly because the obstructions are slight. This is an error because the power is with the weak and what seemed like easy victory is doomed to failure.

Six in the fourth place means:

If one is in the position of giving guidance to a powerful man, there is always a danger of the man taking offence and actual bloodshed arising. It is only by remaining true and sincere that such dangers will not manifest. Then the outcome will be good.

Nine in the fifth place means:

Loyalty will lead to strong bonds between friends. In the weaker person this manifests as devotion, in the stronger as trustworthiness.

Nine at the top means:

Success is at hand but should not be taken for granted. There are still dangers. Do not be tempted to advance further this time, as it would only lead to misfortune.

10 Lü/Treading (Conduct) ☰

Above Ch'ien The Creative, Heaven
Below Tui The Joyous, Lake

The youngest daughter waits upon her father with good humour and does not make him angry. The weak can make a stand against the strong here because the stand is made with good humour and without presumption. In this way the strong person is not irritated.

The meaning

A potentially difficult situation has arisen. The strong is closely followed by the weak. Although the weak could be an encumbrance to the strong, the strong does not harm the weak because the interaction is with good humour and harmless. If you want to deal with strong, difficult people, the only way to achieve success is to behave with decorum. A pleasant manner will calm the irritated person. Tact and diplomacy are called for.

The image

Recognize that your position in life is governed by your inner worth. If you associate with those who recognize this truth, order and harmony will reign.

The lines

Nine at the beginning means:

If you act with quiet confidence and make no demands on others, you will remain free to follow your path. Be happy with where you are and be content to make quiet progress.

Nine in the second place means:

If you are to tread your path free from entanglements, you must tread it like a sage. Ask nothing of anyone, seek nothing and do not be enticed by worldly goals. Remain true to yourself and good fortune will come.

Six in the third place means:

Your powers are not yet strong enough for you to challenge others. Such challenges will lead to misfortune. Reckless forging ahead can be justified only if it is to protect and battle for those whom you love.

Nine in the fourth place means:

Despite your hesitancy, you possess the inner power to win through. You can overcome danger by pressing forwards.

Nine in the fifth place means:

You must be resolute in your actions, but it is only by keeping your eyes open to danger that you will achieve success.

Nine at the top means:

The work is over. It is only by looking back at the consequences of your actions that you can judge whether you have been successful or not. If the effects are good, success will follow.

11 T'ai/Peace ䷊

Above K'un   The Receptive, Earth
Below Ch'ien   The Creative, Heaven

This hexagram is linked to the first month of the Chinese year (February–March), the time when nature prepares to burst into spring bloom. The orientation of the two trigrams, earth above and heaven below, denotes a time when heaven appears to be on earth. Everything is prospering, sprouting and full of life. All in the world is harmonious.

The meaning

This hexagram represents heaven on earth. Peace and harmony abound with everything in its correct place. Positive energies are fully in control. Negative influences are counterbalanced and transformed by this positive energy, allowing peace and harmony to reign. The positive within every situation can be readily found, bringing good fortune and success.

The image

The union of heaven and earth produces an image of peace. This situation can continue only if you align yourself to nature. In this way you will change as the seasons change and will reap the rewards of a rich harvest.

The lines

Nine at the beginning means:

You can accomplish much at this time. It is a time of prosperity of which you should take advantage. You have the ability to be able to attract like-minded people to you while at the same time having a positive influence upon all those you encounter on your path. Take advantage of these favourable influences to achieve something.

Nine in the second place means:

Do not let your own success and the success of those around you go to your head. This is not a time for you to forget or distance yourself from those who are finding life hard at present. It is also not a time to ignore those areas of your life that still require work.

Nine in the third place means:

Everything changes. The euphoria of success will subside and there is a danger that this will lead to melancholy. This does not have to be so. Remain true to yourself, be aware of potential dangers and good fortune will not desert you.

Six in the fourth place means:

Do not boast of your good fortune to those who are less fortunate than you. Pride and arrogance will lead only to your downfall. Treat all you meet with love and humility.

Six in the fifth place means:

It is only through modesty that you will find harmony with others. This will allow you to commune equally with all you meet.

Six at the top means:

The time for good fortune is about to end to be replaced by a time of learning. Embrace this change, as it would lead to opportunities to become wiser. To resist change will lead only to humiliation.

12 P'i/Standstill (Stagnation)

Above Ch'ien   The Creative, Heaven
Below K'un   The Receptive, Earth

This hexagram is the complete reversal of the previous one and represents a time of standstill and decline. It is linked to the seventh month (August–September) when growth has reached its peak and autumn is about to set in.

The meaning

This is a difficult time when those around you who do not tread a righteous path seem to be doing well, while you are achieving little or nothing. Do not lose faith. It is vital that you remain true to your beliefs.

This is a time for seclusion. Being tempted into the world of others will only bring danger.

The image

Those who are not balanced hold the upper hand at present. Have no dealings with them, nor look to them for help. Instead, fall back upon your inner strength and bide your time until conditions change.

The lines

Six at the beginning means:

It would be good to draw others of like mind to one side and wait with them for the winds of change to blow before stepping out again.

Six in the second place means:

Although times are tough, you need to take everything with pleasure and endure this hardship safe in the knowledge that it will not last for ever. This is not a time to mingle with others with a view to drowning your sorrows. By accepting what is happening to you, you will not then compromise your principles.

Six in the third place means:

When the wrong people attain power through ill means, they do not feel equal to the responsibility such powers require. They secretly feel ashamed and although they do not yet outwardly show it, it marks a turn for the better.

Nine in the fourth place means:

The time of change is near. A strong person is needed to restore order. Whoever that person is must be truly called to the task for success to be assured. When such person is found, everyone benefits.

Nine in the fifth place means:

The right person, able to restore order, has arrived. Everything bodes well but this is a time for great caution. As the transition takes place, success is assured only through being watchful at all times.

Nine at the top means:

For the standstill to come to an end, movement must be initiated. For stagnation not to reappear, movement must continue. Keep treading the path set out before you with diligence.

13 T'ung Jên/Fellowship with Others ☰

Above Ch'ien   The Creative, Heaven
Below Li   The Clinging, Flame

This hexagram complements hexagram 7 Shih/The Army. Shih has danger within and obedience without symbolizing many men held together by a strong leader. T'ung Jên, on the other hand, has clarity within and strength without symbolizing a peaceful union of men (people).

The meaning

With the help of those around you, much can be accomplished and this is also a good time to undertake new challenges. For there to be co-operation, there needs to be a leading force that is both persevering and enlightened. People truly work as a team only when they share a common goal. When unity prevails, even the most difficult undertakings can bring forth success.

The image

For fellowship between people to be harmonious, every individual must be valued by all and know its place in the grand scheme of things. Without this, chaos and disharmony will ensue and even the simplest of undertakings will fail.

The lines

Nine at the beginning means:

For you to gain invaluable help from those around you, it is vital that all parties concerned know everything that is going on. Secret agreements will only bring misfortune.

Six in the second place means:

Do not allow egos and personal interests to cause factions to be formed amongst those with whom you work, this will only bring disharmony and humiliation.

Nine in the third place means:

There is danger of mistrust developing in the fellowship and this must be addressed promptly before it breaks the union apart.

Nine in the fourth place means:

Although there have been disagreements, reconciliation is moving nearer. The end to fighting will bring good fortune.

Nine in the fifth place means:

True friendship weathers every storm and takes difficulties and disagreements in its stride knowing that the bond of love is sweet and strong. This ultimately leads to great joy.

Nine at the top means:

Embracing the friendship of others will lead to good fortune.

14 Ta Yu/Great Wealth ☲

Above Li   The Clinging, Flame
Below Ch'ien   The Creative, Heaven

There is a great light shining in the heavens illuminating all things on the earth. The fifth line is a weak line held in a position of honour and is symbolic of the man who has achieved a position of honour, yet at the same time has remained humble and modest.

The meaning

The great light shining in the heavens is symbolic of the sun and indicative of wealth on a grand scale. Such wealth needs to be administered properly. The sun illuminates good and bad, and it is the duty of the wealthy person to be modest and kind and to always turn away from evil towards good. In this way such a person will continue to attract success and good fortune.

The image

The light of the sun brings all things into view. Do not be dazzled by the lure of attractive things. Not all things that look good are good. Only the discerning person who seeks only what is good and right will ultimately find success and happiness.

The lines

Nine at the beginning means:

Wealth has its price and that price is responsibility. The rich person should always be mindful of the potential dangers ahead and must be especially aware of arrogance and wastefulness.

Nine in the second place means:

Wealth of any sort should not be hoarded but put to good use. There are those around you who are honest and responsible enough to be able to help you use your wealth wisely.

Nine in the third place means:

You should regard yourself as possessing nothing as your exclusive, personal property. Be willing to allow your possessions to be used by others who may need them. This includes your spiritual wealth.

Nine in the fourth place means:

When in a position of wealth do not become greedy. Guard against jealousy and envy and your path will be without blame.

Six in the fifth place means:

Things are very favourable. You are attracting many people into your life. Remember to act with dignity in front of others so that they maintain their respect for you.

Nine at the top means:

Walk with beauty, truth and kindness and all will go exceedingly well.

15 Ch'ien/Modesty ☷☶

Above K'un   The Receptive, Earth
Below Kên   Keeping Still, Mountain

This hexagram represents the earth, whose quality is loneliness, being lifted up by the mountain. This is symbolic of a lowly, simple person whose qualities are humility and modesty, being exalted.

The meaning

As sure as the sun rises and sets and the moon waxes and wanes, so too will the modest man be exalted. Wherever you are, whatever your station, always be modest and you will command great respect and achieve good fortune.

The image

The image here is one of finding balance. The wise person reduces that which is too great, and increases that which is too small. In this way all things become equal creating conditions of co-operation and harmony.

The lines

Six at the beginning means:

If one approaches difficulties and obstacles with modesty, making no demands nor holding high expectations, even great barriers can be overcome.

Six in the second place means:

If one maintains a modest attitude, it is reflected in one's outward behaviour. This brings about respect from others and good fortune.

Nine in the third place means:

There is a danger that as you achieve great things, you will lose your modesty. This must be guarded against as it will lose you the support of others and will prevent you from fulfilling your goal.

Six in the fourth place means:

As you progress forwards, maintain your modesty and always have respect for those around you.

Six in the fifth place means:

Modesty should not be confused with a weak will. There are times when you will need to exert your authority. This should be done without arrogance, neither should it cause offence.

Six at the top means:

A modest person needs to look within themselves openly and honestly and should not shy away from dealing with difficult issues.

16 Yü/Enthusiasm ䷏

Above Chên   The Arousing, Thunder
Below K'un   The Receptive, Earth

This hexagram represents a leading official (the fourth strong line) meeting with obedience and devotion from all others (the other five weak lines). This means that if a person conducts her or himself with devotion and respect for the laws of the universe, the path will be easy and all those who help him or her will do so with joy and enthusiasm.

The meaning

This is a good time to undertake new ventures, for if you approach everything with enthusiasm, your enthusiasm will spread to those around you and this will enable you to achieve much.

The image

The image is of the first thunderstorm of summer. Before it comes there is a closeness and tension in the air. The birds and insects are silent, waiting for the tension to be resolved. After the storm the atmosphere notably lifts and all of creation rejoices in a hive of activity. This signifies a time when the best course of action is to be active because all the energies are right for you to succeed.

The lines

Six at the beginning means:

Enthusiasm should never be arrogant or egotistical as this will only lead to misfortune. Enthusiasm is appropriate only when it is the general emotion of a group that unites and inspires all.

Six in the second place means:

Do not let your enthusiasm dazzle you. Remain level headed and always be aware of potential dangers ahead so that you can react to them before they come upon you and throw you off your path.

Six in the third place means:

Do not let contentment blind you to the need to change when appropriate. This is not time for hesitation, seize the moment lest your life be filled with regret.

Nine in the fourth place means:

Step forwards with neither doubt nor fear. Remain sincere and enthusiastic and you will attract the right helpers towards you.

Six in the fifth place means:

Enthusiasm is obstructed and there are constant pressures, but these will actually help to prevent you from becoming complacent.

Six at the top means:

Be wary of over-enthusiasm leading to delusion. If you realize that you have become deluded, all is not lost. You have the opportunity to change and this is very favourable.

17 Sui/Following ䷐

Above Tui   The Joyous, Lake
Below Chên   The Arousing, Thunder

For a person to create a following, he or she needs to arouse interest (Chên) and at the same time bring gladness (Tui). True followers will remain faithful of their own free will only if they are happy.

The meaning

The message here is one of adaptation. To create a following, one must first learn to serve. One cannot obtain a true following through cunning or deception. Whether one is a follower or a leader, one must always adapt to the changes of energy in group situations while at the same time keeping focused on what is right. In this way there will be peace and harmony.

The image

The image is of thunder in the middle of the lake representing a time of darkness and rest. After work comes the need for rest. Tiredness will take away your ability to adapt so allow yourself time for rest and recuperation.

The lines

Nine at the beginning means:

It is important to listen to all the points of view both within and without a group of people while at the same time guarding against compromising your beliefs; just to keep the peace.

Six in the second place means:

Choose your friends wisely. A man cannot serve two masters. You must be wary of spending time in bad company as it will jeopardize your opportunities to learn from wise people.

Six in the third place means:

When one moves forwards, there is always a sense of leaving the past behind and sometimes this means parting company with people who are no longer travelling in the same direction as you. Do not fight this. Remain firm on your path and do not be led astray by others who do not share your vision.

Nine in the fourth place means:

As you grow spiritually, you would naturally attract some people to you who will flatter you in order to use you to gain their own personal advantage. You must be free from ego so that you can see through such people.

Nine in the fifth place means:

If you follow only what is good and beautiful you will meet with great fortune.

Six at the top means:

Keep to a true path and you will form unbreakable bonds with good people who will be of great help and support to you.

18 Ku/Repairing the Damage (Decay) ䷑

Above Kên   Keeping Still, Mountain
Below Sun   The Gentle, Wind

The Chinese character Ku represents a bowl full of breeding worms and has the image of decay. The root cause of the decay must be addressed so this hexagram is entitled 'work on what has been spoiled' or, more literally, 'repairing the damage'.

The meaning

To repair what has become damaged, one must first ascertain the root cause, then decide what action needs to be taken both to repair the damage and to make sure it does not happen again. This is true in cases of external damage (e.g. between friends) or internal damage (e.g. negative character traits).

The image

The image is one of decay. Decay is caused by stagnation. The wind blows on the mountain clearing away the dead and decaying vegetation. The mountain then nourishes the new seedlings. In the same way, a leader sometimes needs to stir up public opinion to remove stagnation and then calm and nourish the people, thus allowing them to grow.

The lines

Six at the beginning means:

Decay has come about through rigid adherence to tradition but has not penetrated deeply and so is easily solved. This does not mean that matters should not be taken seriously. The decay must be addressed now before it spreads.

Nine in the second place means:

Decay has come through weakness and needs to be addressed with gentleness and compassion. Proceeding with too much vigour will only cause further damage.

Nine in the third place means:

If one proceeds to correct mistakes a little too energetically, minor discords will develop in the process. This should not cause great concern because all will end harmoniously. Better too much energy than too little.

Six in the fourth place means:

Damage is coming to the surface that has its roots in the past. You must find the strength to deal with this for if it is allowed to run its course, it will only bring heartache.

Six in the fifth place means:

If you lack the strength to deal with things from the past on your own, seek others to help you initiate the needed change.

Nine at the top means:

Once damage is repaired, it is not a time to rest on your laurels. You must continue to work towards greater understanding and spiritual growth.

19 Lin/Approach ䷒

Above K'un   The Receptive, Earth
Below Tui   The Joyous, Lake

The Chinese word *Lin* has a variety of meanings. The first meaning in the *Book of Changes* is given as 'becoming great'. This is followed by the meaning 'to approach', especially in the context of approaching that which is strong or highly placed. It further includes the concept of one in a high position looking down graciously upon those below.

The meaning

A time of joy and progress is upon you. Spring is just around the corner. This is a good time to act although steadfastness is called for to make full use of the opportunities now presenting themselves. Also, be aware that this time will not last for ever so you must be vigilant. If you can foresee obstacles before they manifest, you will be able to overcome them before they grow to full power.

The image

The earth surrounds the lake in an endless embrace. In the same way a wise man needs to be tireless in his readiness to teach those whom he meets on his path.

The lines

Nine at the beginning means:

This is a good time to join with others in positive works, remembering not to get carried away but always to adhere to what is right.

Nine in the second place means:

Everything on the earth is transitory. For every rise there must follow a fall. The person who understands this and can adjust to these changes will continue to make swift progress and meet good fortune.

Six in the third place means:

Things are going well but at such times there is always a danger of complacency and this must be vigorously resisted.

Six in the fourth place means:

Always remain open-minded and be willing to learn from those who seem to be less advanced than you and good fortune will follow.

Six in the fifth place means:

Great wisdom is called for. Be wise in your selection of the people you ask to help you. Once a choice is made, allow those people the space in which to work without interference.

Six at the top means:

Sometimes, having progressed above and beyond a certain place in one's learning, there is need to return to show others the way. There is no blame in this.

20 Kuan/Contemplation (View) ☷

Above Sun   The Gentle, Wind
Below K'un   The Receptive, Earth

This hexagram has two meanings. The hexagram outlines a simple picture of a tower with the broken lines representing two supports and the unbroken lines the platform. A tower provides a wide view of the surrounding area and is therefore a good place for contemplation and viewing, but it is also visible for miles around and so this hexagram incorporates the sense of being an example to those around you.

The meaning

Through simple living and contemplation, one can begin to understand the underlying workings of the universe. This not only provides a great opportunity for spiritual growth, but also enables one to have a positive influence on those around. Such influence can be achieved only through self-discipline and honesty.

The image

The image is of the wind blowing across the plain and is likened to the king surveying his realm. When a king surveys his realm, he has an opportunity to check that everything is running smoothly throughout his land. Equally when the people see the king, his presence and personality should inspire them. Likewise through contemplation you can check that your path is unfolding smoothly and such actions will have a positive influence on those around you.

The lines

Six at the beginning means:

You have not yet comprehended your current lessons. You must look deeper and harder within yourself.

Six in the second place means:

Be wary not to spend so much time looking within that you lose sight of the world around you and cut yourself off from others. Seek balance at all times.

Six in the third place means:

This is a time of transition. Having gained a degree of self-knowledge you must now put that knowledge to use. Contemplation should not lead to a preoccupation with the self but with an awareness of how your thoughts and actions affect those with whom you come into contact.

Six in the fourth place means:

You can exert a positive influence on others using your new knowledge. With wisdom you will be able to be of help to others without being used or abused.

Nine in the fifth place means:

A time of self-examination is called for. Self-examination should not be about brooding over oneself but about making sure that one's actions and influence are having a positive effect.

Nine at the top means:

If you can master your ego, contemplation can then be directed to perceiving the laws of the universe. This will then give you the wisdom to act always for the highest good.

21 Shih Ho/Biting Through ䷔

Above Li The Clinging, Fire
Below Chên The Arousing, Thunder

The top and bottom lines of this hexagram represent the lips, with the broken lines representing teeth. The fourth unbroken line represents an obstruction in the mouth that prevents the lips from meeting. This obstruction must be bitten through for there to be union.

The meaning

An obstruction has manifested which will not disappear with time but must be dealt with for union and harmony to come about. Furthermore, the obstruction must be dealt with in the correct manner for success to be assured. This is a time for neither hardness nor over-excitement. Calmness and gentle but firm action are required. Clear thinking will allow you to remove the obstruction without causing yourself harm or imbalance.

The image

The image is one of clarity and purpose. You need to have a clear sense of where you want to go and not to allow obstructions to deter you from your path and goals.

The lines

Nine at the beginning means:

If someone is obstructing you for the first time, gentle actions will enable him or her to see their error and to resume their right path. Thus the obstruction on your path will be removed.

Six in the second place means:

There is a danger of going a bit too far in your removal of an obstruction, but there is no blame in this as your actions are justified.

Six in the third place means:

The issue is an old one and will not be removed without some difficulties. This means that you need to look deep within yourself to find the solution you are seeking.

Nine in the fourth place means:

The obstacles presenting themselves on your path at present are great. They require strength, clear actions and perseverance to be overcome. If approached in this way, success will be achieved.

Six in the fifth place means:

Things need to be approached with objectivity. Keep in mind the possible dangers on the way to avoid making mistakes.

Nine at the top means:

You are not listening to warnings and your obstinacy could lead to misfortune.

22 Pi/Grace ䷕

Above Kên   Keeping Still, Mountain
Below Li   The Clinging, Fire

For any union to be harmonious, grace is required. This means that all actions and thoughts should be beautiful and come from a perspective of love.

The meaning

Those who act with grace can achieve a great success although grace is not an essential ingredient for success and therefore should be used sparingly.

The image

Fire illuminates the mountain making it pleasing to the eye with its shimmering beauty. This is a nice way to view the world but does not give the whole perspective. Do not accept that which appears to be on the surface as the whole picture. Earnestly seek the truth.

The lines

Nine at the beginning means:

At the beginning of any endeavour, hard work is the only way to assure success. Do not seek short-cuts, as at this stage they will only lead to an imperfect outcome.

Six in the second place means:

Seeking to look beautiful on the outside while not addressing any internal issues is vanity and will only lead to misfortune.

Nine in the third place means:

When things are going smoothly, do not be lulled into a false sense of security. Complacency must never be allowed to replace perseverance if success is to be assured.

Six in the fourth place means:

There is a bright path ahead beckoning you. Do not allow its charm to woo you, for it is a path of enslavement. Return to the path of simplicity, for it is the only one that leads to freedom.

Six in the fifth place means:

It appears that the simple path you have chosen is not rewarding you as much as the paths of those who seek riches and luxury. This is an illusion. Remain sincere and you will find riches beyond measure.

Nine at the top means:

True grace comes not from ornamentation, but from simplicity of form. Seek always the simplest path and grace will find you.

23 Po/Splitting Apart ☶

Above Kên   Keeping Still, Mountain
Below K'un   The Receptive, Earth

The weak, broken lines have gained enough power to split the last strong line. This is not done by direct actions, but by a gradual undermining of the foundations leading ultimately to collapse. This hexagram represents the ninth month (October–November), the time when the power of the cold is about to reign supreme over the power of the sun.

The meaning

When winter storms are raging, work on the land must cease. So, too, at this time of difficulty one must learn acceptance and remain quiet. Everything has a beginning, middle and end. This time will pass and spring will once again return. To submit and avoid action at this time is not cowardice but wisdom.

The image

The mountain that does not have firm foundations will eventually topple over. Likewise in all your endeavours, for success to be assured, it is essential that the groundwork and preparation be carried out correctly. In this way success will not be fleeting but will endure.

The lines

Six at the beginning means:

Negative forces are trying to undermine your good works. The situation seems hopeless. Learn acceptance and live in the present for there is nothing you can do but wait.

Six in the second place means:

The powers of the negative forces around you are growing stronger. Extreme caution is called for. Stubborn resistance or trying to make a stand for what you believe in will only cause you harm. Although you may feel isolated at present, have patience. This time will not last for ever.

Six in the third place means:

Do not compromise your truth. If it brings you into opposition with others there is no blame in this.

Six in the fourth place means:

The negative forces have reached their peak and can no longer be warded off.

Six in the fifth place means:

Here the situation has changed. Instead of the negative forces undermining the strong, they are actually opening up a path towards the strong that will ultimately lead to happiness and fulfilment. This is very positive.

Nine at the top means:

Misfortune has reached its end and better times are returning. Spring brings new hope and growth after the cold desolation of winter. All goes well.

24 Fu/Return (The Turning Point) ䷗

Above K'un   The Receptive, Earth
Below Chên   The Arousing, Thunder

This hexagram is linked to the eleventh month in the Chinese calendar (December–January), the time of the Winter Solstice. The Winter Solstice marks the turning point of the year. From then on the power of the darkness is receding and the power of the light is growing.

The meaning

After a time of darkness, the light that was banished now returns. This brings natural movement after a time of stillness and contemplation and marks a time of renewal and transformation. The tiniest piece of light has the power to banish the darkness and this signifies a time of releasing the old and embracing the new. This is a nodal point when negative turns to positive and disharmony to harmony.

The image

The image is of thunder in the earth symbolizing the beginning of movement. The thunder is still underground though so this is not a time of great action. In China, the Winter Solstice is a day of rest and this is carried forwards in the meaning of this hexagram. Although there is some movement, it needs consolidating by rest. This will allow the movement to gather momentum until it has the power to burst into action. Do not try to push things, allow all things to unfold. New projects need to be nurtured or they will not reach fruition. This is a time of beginnings and requires wisdom and patience if success is to be assured.

The lines

Nine at the beginning:

When negative thoughts enter the mind, they must be banished immediately. There should be no guilt in having such thoughts as they are part of life's learning process but they should never be allowed to take root and grow within the mind.

Six in the second place means:

Do not allow pride to stop you learning from others. Choose your allies wisely and they will show you many lessons.

Six in the third place means:

You must learn to 'walk your talk'. Continually giving in to uncontrollable desires will only bring misfortune. Continue to strive for what is good and right.

Six in the fourth place means:

Do not spend your time with imbalanced people. Choose to be with strong and good friends and all will go well.

Six in the fifth place means:

Examine yourself honestly. If you have wronged another, resolve to redress matters immediately. This will bring no regret.

Six at the top means:

If you are obstinate and maintain an unhealthy attitude to life, this will only bring misfortune upon you. A change of attitude is immediately called for.

25 Wu Wang/Innocence (The Unexpected) ䷘

Above Ch'ien   The Creative, Heaven
Below Chên   The Arousing, Thunder

The trigram Chên below is under the strong influence of Ch'ien above symbolizing the man who follows the guidance of the heavenly (spiritual) without question. This is like the child who follows the path set out before it without question, hence this hexagram is called 'Innocence'. Such actions lead one on a journey into the unknown and so this hexagram also symbolizes the unexpected.

The meaning

We are all born with a sense of what is good and right. By devoting oneself to spiritual development, one learns that intuition can bring an instinctive surety to one's path that, in turn, brings success and rewards. Align yourself to nature. Seek to live naturally as a spiritual being and never lose your connection to the divine and all will go well. If you lose your connection to heaven, your intuition can then mislead you and this will only bring misfortune.

The image

The image is of springtime when the buds open and the world is full of vitality. Everything is new and fresh and the power of creation is at its strongest. All things know when to grow because they are under the influence of heaven. In the same way, a wise person draws upon their spiritual wealth so that all their thoughts and actions are timed to perfection.

The lines

Nine at the beginning means:

Follow your first instinct as it comes from your heart and is always good. Be assured and confident and success will come.

Six in the second place means:

Live in the present and perform every task with pleasure giving each one your best efforts. Give to everything the time and effort it deserves and all undertakings will succeed.

Six in the third place means:

Occasionally, apparently undeserved misfortune befalls us. This occurs so that we can learn to be wiser and stronger. In all undertakings, no matter how small, you should give your undivided attention if you do not wish advantage to be taken of you.

Nine in the fourth place means:

Do not try to cling to belongings, for even if you lose something, it still belongs to you and so should cause you no concern. Your only concern should be remaining true to yourself and to allow your spiritual path to unfold before you.

Nine in the fifth place means:

If an unexpected obstacle or negative energy comes your way, it is not from you nor is it part of you, so you need give it no thought. Do not waste your energy in trying to forcibly remove it, just allow nature to take its course and it will pass by itself.

Nine at the top means:

Do not try to force issues, as this will only bring misfortune. When the time is not ripe for progress to be made, the only sensible course of action is to wait quietly and patiently.

26 Ta Ch'u/The Taming Power of the Great ䷙

Above Kên   Keeping Still, Mountain
Below Ch'ien   The Creative, Heaven

This hexagram is a direct contrast to hexagram 9, Hsiao Ch'u, The Taming Power of the Small where five strong lines were held in check by one weak line. In this hexagram there are four strong lines held in check by two weak lines providing a stronger restraining power, hence The Taming Power of the Great.

The meaning

The wise man renews his commitment to following a spiritual path on a daily basis. There is great potential power to be harnessed but this can be achieved only through strict adherence to what is good and right. If this is done, difficult and challenging undertakings will be assured of success.

The image

The image is of heaven held within the mountain symbolizing hidden treasures. These hidden treasures are lessons to be learnt from the past. The past is just a memory and can serve no other purpose than to instruct and teach wisdom. If viewed in this way, you will be able to let the past go, live in the present and look forward to the fulfilment of your dreams.

The lines

Nine at the beginning means:

If you have met an obstacle on your path, do not try to force an advance, as this will only bring misfortune. Learn to wait with patience, renew your energies and the solution will manifest.

Nine in the second place means:

This is a time for consolidating your energies and waiting until the right time for movement returns. Trying to force issues will only deplete your energy and this will then stop you from making the best progress when the time for movement returns.

Nine in the third place means:

The obstacle is cleared and the way ahead is now open. Proceed with strength and determination, but remain cautious, as there are still potential dangers ahead that will take you off your path if you are not alert to them.

Six in the fourth place means:

Foresight is called for so that you can pre-empt dangers and forestall them before they cause you harm. This will bring good fortune.

Six in the fifth place means:

When dangers manifest, do not meet them head-on, but look for the root cause and all will go well.

Nine at the top means:

All obstacles are clear and the path ahead is straight and sure. This is the reward for your patience and steadfastness.

27 I/The Corners of the Mouth (Providing Nourishment) ䷚

Above Kên   Keeping Still, Mountain
Below Chên   The Arousing, Thunder

This hexagram forms a picture of an open mouth with the top and bottom lines forming the lips. The mouth is the place through which we take our nourishment in the form of food and so this hexagram is symbolic of providing nourishment.

The meaning

The body is the vehicle for the soul and it is vital that we seek to take the best possible care of it. One can tell a great deal about an individual by observing how he nourishes himself. A man who feeds only his ego will ultimately be unfulfilled. Integration between the body, mind and spirit is totally dependent upon each part of one's being receiving the correct nourishment. If any part is not properly fed, the whole being suffers.

The image

Thunder at the foot of the mountain brings nourishment to the land. For one to be properly nourished, one needs to give and receive food with peace and tranquillity. Eating and drinking is receiving food and it can be properly digested only if one consumes it in a calm and tranquil state. Likewise, our words provide spiritual nourishment to others and should be given with the same calm and tranquil intent.

The lines

Nine at the beginning means:

Be content with your own path and seek your own nourishment. Do not be envious of those who appear outwardly better off than you as this will corrupt your mind and only bring misfortune.

Six in the second place means:

Poor nourishment brings weakness of spirit and leads to misfortune. It is your responsibility to nourish yourself. If you always seek nourishment from others, you will lose your power.

Six in the third place means:

Self-gratification leads to unwanted desires. The indiscriminate pursuit of pleasure for personal satisfaction will never bring you your dreams. Nothing good can come from such actions.

Six in the fourth place means:

You are hungry for the type of success that will be of benefit to everyone. There is no wrong in this. Seek help from the right people and all will go well.

Six in the fifth place means:

You do not have the strength yet to help others and you need to seek the guidance of a wise, but humble person. If you persevere on this path, you will eventually find the strength you need to succeed, but you must be mindful of not trying to run before you can walk.

Nine at the top means:

You have the strength and wisdom to make your dreams reality and this will be to the benefit of all. Your responsibility is to seek only those things that make you happy, healthy and fulfilled. This is a good time to embark upon difficult undertakings.

28 Ta Kuo/Preponderance of the Great

Above Tui   The Joyous, Lake
Below Sun   The Gentle, Wind

The outside two lines weaken the four strong lines and if the situation is not resolved, collapse will occur bringing great misfortune. This situation must either pass or be changed.

The meaning

You have taken on more than you can handle. You are too weak for the heavy responsibilities that are now manifesting in your life. Take action immediately to remedy this situation or it will be to your detriment. Your core is strong though; so you need have no fear. You must use this strength to gently initiate change. Do not try to use forcible measures but instead gentle persistence.

The image

The image is of the water rising above the trees but this situation is not permanent. A strong man stands alone and undaunted when all around him fall. Rely upon your inner strength and you will prevail.

The lines

Six at the beginning means:

Any undertaking at this time will succeed only if it is handled with extreme caution and care. Make sure its foundations are firm and that all possible dangers have been foreseen.

Nine in the second place means:

Although the present situation is unusual, it is not bad and provided you keep to your path, all will go well.

Nine in the third place means:

You are blindly plunging ahead without giving heed to the warnings of others. This will only bring misfortune and, if not averted, will end in disaster.

Nine in the fourth place means:

Do not misuse the power you possess to get yourself free from the present situation. Only honesty and integrity will bring success.

Nine in the fifth place means:

Do not seek to distance yourself from the support of others, as this will only deplete your energy and lead to imbalance.

Six at the top means:

If the opposition is too strong, there is no blame in giving up for the time being. Trying to force your dreams will only lead to misfortune. Nothing is for ever and as soon as things change, you will be able to refocus on your dream.

29 K'an/The Abysmal (Water) ☵

Above K'an   The Abysmal, Water
Below K'an   The Abysmal, Water

The doubling of the trigram K'an signifies great danger, the solution to which can only be found through objectivity and awareness.

The meaning

One needs to become accustomed to the dangers about so that they do not daunt one. Just as the flowing water always finds its way out of the ravine, so too will you find safe passage. Do not shrink from danger but face it with confidence and fearlessness trusting in your own path to carry you through. If you approach things with an open and honest heart, you will find success. The solution to any problem comes from changing the perspective by which you view that problem. Danger is not a bad thing, it is how you react to it that is good or bad. Properly used, danger can sharpen your senses and protect you from harm.

The image

The image is of water flowing on uninterrupted. When water is flowing down a ravine, it fills up every empty space before it flows on in its persistent path forwards. You must remain consistent and true if you are to safely reach your goal.

The lines

Six at the beginning means:

In becoming accustomed to danger, one can become complacent and this will bring misfortune.

Nine in the second place means:

Just because you are faced with danger does not mean that you should act rashly to try to get out of it. Whenever one is faced with danger, one should first take time to accustom to it so that one can best see the safest course through it.

Six in the third place means:

No matter where you step, you will place yourself in danger. The paths back and forth are fraught with perils so the only thing to do is to remain still and wait until a solution manifests.

Six in the fourth place means:

Do not try to change things with superficial actions. It is only by remaining sincere and by doing only what is required that you will free yourself from the present danger.

Nine in the fifth place means:

Do not be over-ambitious. Choose the path of least resistance and you will achieve your goal. The only priority at present is to get out of danger.

Six at the top means:

Your own irresponsible actions have brought this danger upon you and only you alone are responsible for the prison you presently find yourself in. This does mean, however, that you have the power to ultimately find freedom.

30 Li/The Clinging, Fire ䷝

Above Li   The Clinging, Fire
Below Li   The Clinging, Fire

The doubling of the trigram Li is symbolic of the radiance of nature. Fire has no definite form but is given form by that which it touches. In the same way, the fire of growth and light is formless but is manifest in the beauty of nature in bloom.

The meaning

Adhere to what is right and seek only truth. You are reliant upon the earth for your support and nourishment and learning acceptance that you are dependent upon the earth will help you to align yourself to nature and thus travel smoothly upon your path.

The image

The image is of the doubling of fire representing the need for light to shine in even the darkest places. To reach an enlightenment, you must persevere and allow the truth to enter and shine in the deepest parts of your being.

The lines

Nine at the beginning means:

At the beginning of any endeavour, it is vital that you do not allow yourself to be swept along by the tide of emerging ideas. Remain composed and allow the ideas to flow into you rather than stepping forth to seek them. Without a good and firm beginning, there can be no successful outcome.

Six in the second place means:

Everything is proceeding well and by remaining true and seeking only the highest good, success is assured.

Nine in the third place means:

Because life is transitory, there is a danger of seeking instant gratification or of becoming disillusioned. Both paths are wrong. Remain constant and true and you will reap as you sow.

Nine in the fourth place means:

Do not let over-enthusiasm deplete your energies at the outset of an undertaking, as this will put you in danger of burning yourself out and thus will prevent you from achieving your goal. It is only through perseverance that true success can come.

Six in the fifth place means:

The situation calls for a radical change of attitude if success is to be assured. Remain clear and focused and do not let negative emotions take hold of you.

Nine at the top means:

Learn to change yourself at your core rather than concentrating on superficialities. Do not be overly hard on yourself for your minor failings; instead concentrate on changing your fundamental weaknesses into strengths.

31 Hsien/Influence (Wooing) ䷞

Above Tui **The Joyous, Lake**
Below Kên **Keeping Still, Mountain**

The lower trigram Kên, through its quiet persistence, has a positive influence upon the upper trigram Tui, manifesting as joyousness. This is symbolic of the union between woman and man bringing joy and harmony.

The meaning

Because the path is opening before you, you are attracting good things into your life. Integration is required between the joyous exterior and the calm interior so that you do not let outward joy swell to excess and upset the inner calm that keeps you focused on your path.

The image

The image is of a mountain with a lake at its summit. Such a mountain does not have a pointed peak and is nourished by the water creating harmony and growth. This is symbolic of not getting above one's station but of always seeking humility and sincerity in all your dealings with others.

The lines

Six at the beginning means:

Things are beginning to move although those around you may not recognize this yet. This should be of no concern.

Six in the second place means:

You are being tempted to act before the time is right. Resist this and wait patiently until you are impelled to move by genuine influences.

Nine in the third place means:

Do not act on the spur of the moment. Bide your time and assess all possible outcomes before deciding the correct path.

Nine in the fourth place means:

The only way you can have positive influence over others is by maintaining a true and honest heart. Trying to manipulate others for your own ends will only lead to misfortune.

Nine in the fifth place means:

Maintain a strong will holding firm to what you believe, but do not let this attitude exclude you from the positive influence of others. It is only by allowing yourself to be positively influenced by others that you can have a positive influence on the world around you.

Six at the top means:

Do not regard the influence of words as highly as the influence of actions.

32 Hêng/Duration ䷟

Above Chên   The Arousing, Thunder
Below Sun   The Gentle, Wind

This hexagram is the inverse of the preceding one. When thunder comes, so too does wind and so this hexagram describes a union (between thunder and wind) that endures. This hexagram represents marriage as the enduring union between man and woman.

The meaning

Duration means ongoing movement, not standstill or regression. This is symbolic of maintaining your progress upon your unfolding path. Everything is developing and progressing unhindered by outside influences. Just as summer follows spring and winter follows autumn, if you align yourself to nature, your path too will naturally unfold before you.

The image

Although the rolling thunder and the blowing wind do not endure for ever, the laws governing their coming and going do. This creates the image of duration, for although the thunder stops and the wind calms, both will return again when the time is right. In the same manner, as you tread your path through life, many things come and go, but if you recognize this, nothing can take you off your path of your unfolding destiny.

The lines

Six at the beginning means:

For something to endure, it must be created through diligence and perseverance. Do not attempt too much too soon or your actions will produce no lasting effect.

Nine in the second place means:

If you rely upon your inner strength to carry you through, you will have no cause for remorse.

Nine in the third place means:

Remain consistent. Do not let outside influences dictate your mood as this will only lead to humiliation and sadness.

Nine in the fourth place means:

If you are seeking something, persistence is not enough. You can persistently look for something in the wrong place and never find it. Be wise in your searching. What is not sought in the correct manner will never be found.

Six in the fifth place means:

There is a time to conform and a time to stand alone and do what is right.

Six at the top means:

Do not be impatient or restless, as this will potentially lead you into danger.

33 Tun/Retreat ䷠

Above Ch'ien   The Creative, Heaven
Below Kên   Keeping Still, Mountain

The dark is rising and the light retreats. This is the law of nature and therefore retreat is the correct course of action so that one does not waste one's energy. This hexagram is linked to the sixth month (July–August) when, in China, the first signs of the approaching winter are already manifesting.

The meaning

Negative forces are in the ascendant so retreat is the only right course of action. Retreat does not mean fleeing for one's life. It means an ordered and methodical withdrawal of your energy. On the battlefield, retreat is the precursor to counter-attack and you must make sure that, as you retreat, you keep facing those forces that are against you so that they do not overtake you. The art of constructive retreat is not easy to learn, but perseverance will bring you success.

The image

The image is of a mountain trying to reach up to heaven, with heaven remaining distant and untouchable. This image is a metaphor for how you should act to guard against the encroaching negative energy. You should be like heaven, free from judgement or malice, but untouchable. In this way you will not waste your energy by becoming involved in conflict.

The lines

Six at the beginning means:

This is a time for keeping still, not for action. Do not undertake any new ventures until the climate changes.

Six in the second place means:

Hold fast in your search for truth and you will reach your goal.

Nine in the third place means:

Those around you are resistant to your retreat. The only thing to do is to persuade them to retreat with you. In this way you will not lose control of the situation.

Nine in the fourth place means:

Embrace this retreat with open arms. If you allow yourself to adjust to the changes that retreat brings then nothing can harm you.

Nine in the fifth place means:

The time for retreat is now, but you must keep focused and firm in your decision or you will become side-tracked by irrelevant issues.

Nine at the top means:

The path is clear before you. All you need to do is walk it and you will achieve success.

34 Ta Chuang/The Power of the Great ䷡

Above Chên   The Arousing, Thunder
Below Ch'ien   The Creative, Heaven

This hexagram is linked to the second Chinese month (March–April). The four strong lines have entered the hexagram from below and are rising up with a strong and firm foundation, hence the name 'The Power of the Great'.

The meaning

Your inner power is rising but you must guard against over-confidence. Do not let the fact that you are coming into your power make you forget to seek help and guidance from outside of yourself when necessary. There is also a danger that this power will make you impatient for more movement in your life. Remember, everything comes in its own time and trying to force issues in this situation will lead to disharmony.

The image

The image is of the thunder at springtime symbolizing the power of nature advancing in accordance with the laws of the universe. Everything is as it should be but you must always follow a right and true path. Do not do anything that does not flow with the natural order or disharmony will enter your life.

The lines

Nine at the beginning means:

Part of you wants to press forward, but at this time such action would be a mistake because all of you is not integrated to move forwards in harmony.

Nine in the second place means:

The path is opening before you and you can make great progress. Avoid over-confidence and be ever mindful of maintaining your inner balance.

Nine in the third place means:

Remain humble and ever aware of danger. Just because your power is manifesting does not mean that you can become complacent.

Nine in the fourth place means:

If you quietly persevere with your attempts to overcome the obstacles that present themselves to you, they will eventually crumble and you will overcome them all. In this way you draw on your internal power rather than external force.

Six in the fifth place means:

When you met with resistance, your stubborn desire to make progress kept you on your path. Now that the resistance has gone, it is time to release the stubborn part of your nature as you no longer have need of it.

Six at the top means:

Pressing forward with too much enthusiasm can lead to entanglements where you cannot make progress forwards or back. If you realise this situation and accept it, all will be resolved.

35 Chin/Progress ☲

Above Li   The Clinging, Fire
Below K'un   The Receptive, Earth

This hexagram represents the rising sun in the morning. In nature this is a time of great activity and so this hexagram is symbolic of rapid, easy progress. The sun is also linked to clarity of vision.

The meaning

The opportunity is here to make great progress upon your path but this can be achieved only if you maintain respect for yourself and those around you.

The image

The image is of the sun rising over the earth. During the hours of daylight, it is only the clouds that can mask the light of the sun. This acts as a warning. Although everything appears good, one must always guard against one's judgement being clouded by earthly things.

The lines

Six at the beginning means:

Although everything is in place for rapid forward progress, there are still fears of obstacles ahead. The only course of action is to carry on doing what is right and to remain balanced at all costs.

Six in the second place means:

Progress is interrupted and this brings sadness. The correct course of action is to persevere and maintain a clear intent on where you are heading. In this way progress and happiness will soon return.

Six in the third place means:

You are making progress that is fuelled by the support and encouragement of others. There is no cause for regret that you are not progressing solely by your own power. Everything is as it is meant to be.

Nine in the fourth place means:

Because you are making good progress, there is a danger that you will squander your resources on accumulating possessions. This goes against what is true and right and will only lead you into danger.

Six in the fifth place means:

Although you have an opportunity to be of great influence, it is only through gentleness and quiet reserve that you will find true success. Do not worry about minor gains or losses, the important thing is to remain true to yourself.

Nine at the top means:

When those around you are misguided, it is sometimes appropriate to go on the offensive and to speak your truth. In this way mistakes will be avoided. On the other hand, trying to correct those who do not walk with you will only lead to humiliation.

36 Ming I/Darkening of the Light ☷☲

Above K'un   The Receptive, Earth
Below Li   The Clinging, Fire

This hexagram is the exact opposite of the previous one and is representative of the sun just after it has set. The hexagram literally means 'wounding of the bright' because the power and influence of the sun upon the earth have greatly diminished.

The meaning

To make progress at this time, you must keep the truth within yourself as your inner guiding light while at the same time be yielding and adaptive to outside influences. In this way you can overcome anything.

The image

The image is one of encroaching darkness. Remain cautious and reserved. Do not be side-tracked by the delusions of others and at the same time do not try to show the truth to those that are not ready to see it.

The lines

Nine at the beginning means:

This is a difficult time and you are challenged to hold fast to your dreams despite the fact that those around you do not understand your actions and therefore speak and think ill of you. This should have no effect upon you.

Six in the second place means:

Hindrances and difficulties abound. If you remain selfless and concentrate upon helping those around you, all will be well.

Nine in the third place means:

The root of your obstruction manifests and is overcome. This bodes well but do not be over-eager to press ahead hastily.

Six in the fourth place means:

Understanding the root cause of the darkness allows you to realize that progress cannot be made. You are therefore able to leave the situation before a conflict breaks out.

Six in the fifth place means:

Running away from danger will serve no purpose. Redouble your inner resolve to remain true to yourself and face the world without fear, safe in the knowledge that you will prevail.

Six at the top means:

The darkness is at its strongest, but this inevitably will lead to its defeat.

37 Chia Jên/The Family (The Clan) ䷤

Above Sun   The Gentle, Wind
Below Li   The Clinging, Fire

This hexagram is representative of the harmonious energies of a balanced family being transferred to the outside world. The top line represents the father as a strong leader and protector.

The meaning

A harmonious family is dependent upon balanced relationships between all members. The husband and wife maintain mutual love and respect for each other. The children allow themselves to be guided by the wisdom and experience of their parents while developing their own personalities. When a family is in order, all their dealings with the world are ordered.

The image

The image is of the wind coming from fire. Fire generates energy and is representative of external influence coming from inward action. For the external influence to carry forward, one must 'walk the talk' every hour of every day.

The lines

Nine at the beginning means:

A family without order is disharmonious and disordered. For a family to work together, the children must be taught to follow the order of the universe from the outset. In this way, whims and passing passions in the developing children will not cause long-term disharmony.

Six in the second place means:

Do not try to use force to get what you want. Know your place in the order of things, walk the path set out before you and you will attain your dreams.

Nine in the third place means:

Setting firm boundaries allows those within them to enjoy freedom without attracting danger.

Six in the fourth place means:

Harmony prevails within a family when outgoings and incomings are balanced. So it is with life, do not be always giving out your energy, but allow yourself time for nourishment and to replenish your energies.

Nine in the fifth place means:

If you work from a perspective of love, no one will fear you and yet your influence will be strong.

Nine at the top means:

You will be judged by your actions and intent, and you will gain respect only if you remain balanced and loving.

38 K'uei/Opposition ☲

Above Li   The Clinging, Fire
Below Tui   The Joyous, Lake

Fire meets the lake and creates the image of opposition.

The meaning

You cannot make swift progress in the face of opposition. It is only through small actions that you will have influence. Trying to use force in order to make progress will lead only to misfortune. When the opposition takes the form of two forces at opposite poles (e.g. heaven and earth, male and female, etc.) this represents a great opportunity because when opposites are reconciled, great creativity and harmony can be achieved.

The image

The image is of fire above and the lake below. Fire and water do not mix. When they exist in the same place, they always retain their own characteristics. So, too, must you retain your own character and not let it be influenced detrimentally by opposite energies.

The lines

Nine at the beginning means:

Even in the face of opposition and difficulties, if you avoid making mistakes, all will go well. Do not go chasing dreams in the face of opposition. Remain steadfast and true and your dreams will come to you.

Nine in the second place means:

Because of miscommunications, it is impossible for you to formally resolve disagreements.

Six in the third place means:

It may seem as if everything is conspiring against you and that everywhere you turn you meet opposition and insults. Do not allow these external forces to have influence on you. Remain true and all will be well.

Nine in the fourth place means:

If all around you are imbalanced, you must remain for the time being in isolation. If, on the other hand, you meet someone who thinks and feels the same as you, there is no longer a need for isolation. Kinship with such a person will allow you to achieve your aims.

Six in the fifth place means:

Because you are surrounded by estrangement, you may well not recognize a kindred spirit when it first manifests into your life. Once it shows its true nature to you, it will become a firm ally.

Nine at the top means:

You are being defensive against those around you through misunderstandings. The root cause of these misunderstandings lies within you. Once you realize this and change your inner attitude, harmony will return.

39 Chien/Obstruction ䷦

Above K'an   The Abysmal, Water
Below Kên   Keeping Still, Mountain

This hexagram forms a picture of a deep abyss before you and a steep mountain behind. Obstruction is all around but the emphasis is on overcoming the obstruction.

The meaning

A seemingly impassable obstruction is met and the only course of action is retreat from the impending danger. This only serves as a preparation for overcoming, though. If you seek the alliance of like-minded people and join them under firm leadership, you will be able, with their help, to overcome the obstruction.

The image

The image is of water on the mountain blocking the path forward. The only course of action is to look within for the solution. Sitting down and feeling sorry for yourself will only bring further misery. This situation has the potential to teach you great things if you use introspection to search for the answer.

The lines

Six at the beginning means:

When faced with danger, retreat is the best course of action so that you can objectively assess the situation. In this way you will see clearly how and when to proceed.

Six in the second place means:

Generally one should not meet obstructions head-on, but follow the line of least resistance. In this situation, obstructions are all around so the only way forward is to forge ahead undaunted.

Nine in the third place means:

Do not forge ahead alone. Those around you do not have the strength to follow you. Turn back and consolidate your strength.

Six in the fourth place means:

Again, you cannot forge ahead alone. Wait and renew your bonds with those around you. Then you will be able to join forces to overcome the obstruction.

Nine in the fifth place means:

Do not try to evade obstructions. If you embrace everything with pleasure, you will naturally attract the help you need from others to overcome all difficulties.

Six at the top means:

The obstructions that lie before you tempt you to turn your back on the world, but this would be a mistake. Firm alliances will bring good fortune.

40 Hsieh/Deliverance

Above Chên   **The Arousing, Thunder**
Below K'an   **The Abysmal, Water**

The danger is over, the obstacle removed. Deliverance is a process and this hexagram describes that process.

The meaning

The time of obstruction is over. It is time for you to return to the normal way that you run your life. If there are any unresolved issues, these need to be sorted out as quickly and efficiently as possible. Trying to press ahead too eagerly will bring misfortune.

The image

The image is of the rains and thunder bringing a release of tension and refreshment to the land. Just as the thunder dies away, so you need to let go of the past and allow the future to unfold before you. Do not dwell on past mistakes, but learn from them and allow that wisdom to empower you in the here and now.

The lines

Six at the beginning means:

Now that the obstruction is past, you need to allow yourself time to recuperate in the new atmosphere of peace and quiet.

Nine in the second place means:

By maintaining your focus, the obstacles and hindrances that have blocked your path have allowed you to build a great deal of inner strength. This can now be put to good use to further you along your path allowing you to brush aside falsehoods and deceptions.

Six in the third place means:

Now that conditions have changed, there is a danger that you are tempted to sit back on your laurels. Such action will only bring misfortune.

Nine in the fourth place means:

During the time of standstill, you have made acquaintances with those who could hold you back. Because the obstruction is now clear, you must press forwards, leaving behind those who are not ready or able to walk with you.

Six in the fifth place means:

Deliverance does not come through external events, but through you learning to break free of negative influences within your own mind.

Six at the top means:

You have the power within yourself to break free and you must seize that power now. Step forwards with confidence and surety. In this way you will be able to be released from the negative influences that have dogged your path recently.

41 Sun/Decrease ䷨

Above Kên   Keeping Still, Mountain
Below Tui   The Joyous, Lake

This hexagram describes a situation where there is a shift of power that has potential to cause instability, but it also offers insights into how to shift the balance without causing instability.

The meaning

Decrease and increase are neither positive nor negative; they are just states of existence. How you adjust to the changing situation dictates whether its effects are for good or ill. At this time of decrease you need to look to simplify your life and to rely upon your inner strength to see you through. You should not try to cover up the fact that you are experiencing a time of decrease, for this would only serve to weaken you.

The image

The image is of a lake at the foot of a mountain with its water evaporating, hence the image of decrease. The mountain symbolizes stubborn strength and the lake is symbolic of uncontrolled gaiety. Both of these emotions if allowed to grow in power unchecked will lead to imbalance. This is why decrease is vital at this time because it will necessitate a need for restriction that will, in turn, bring focus and clarity.

The lines

Nine at the beginning means:

It is good and right for you, after learning from an experience, to direct your energies to helping others with love and humility. You must, however, judge very carefully how much help you give because if you make solutions too easy for others, they may not learn everything they need to from that experience.

Nine in the second place means:

To help another person to the detriment of your own well-being is wrong. You must keep a high degree of self-awareness in your dealings with others to guard against this.

Six in the third place means:

When three people work together, jealousy may rise up resulting in one of the party having to leave. A true bond can take place only between two people, not three. Similarly, if you are alone, you will attract a companion to complement your energy.

Six in the fourth place means:

Your own inner failings prevent people from getting close to you, but if you humbly address these faults and resolve them, those who want to get close to you will embrace you with open arms.

Six in the fifth place means:

If it is your destiny to have good fortune, nothing and no one can take that away from you.

Nine at the top means:

If you persevere with your path, it will be of great benefit not only to you, but to all whom you meet.

42 I/Increase ☳

Above Sun   **The Gentle, Wind**
Below Chên   **The Arousing, Thunder**

The idea expressed in this hexagram is one of increase. The strong lowest line of the upper trigram has sunk to the lowest line of the lower trigram, conveying the sense of sacrifice in the upper trigram leading to an increase in power to the lower trigram.

The meaning

If someone in a high position makes a sacrifice that is of benefit to all, it fills the community with joy and a sense of well-being. The people grow in their devotion to their leader and this creates a sense of cohesion and co-operation that facilitates the successful undertaking of even difficult tasks. This is a good and auspicious time to launch new projects or to face challenges. You can make very effective use of your time at present and you need to take advantage of this, as this time of increase will not last for ever.

The image

The image is of wind and thunder stirring everything up and increasing and strengthening each other. This denotes a time when you can make great progress upon your path by strengthening your weaknesses and releasing negativity. Take advantage of this time to make yourself better, stronger and wiser.

The lines

Nine at the beginning means:

This is a time when much can be achieved, but it is only by remaining selfless that you will truly be able to take advantage of this.

Six in the second place means:

If you approach undertakings with an open and honest heart, the things you are striving for must inevitably come to pass. When your intent is in harmony with heaven, even accidents and obstacles will not deter you provided that you are alert to these potential dangers.

Six in the third place means:

This is such an auspicious time that even things that you may have in the past perceived as negative will have a positive outcome. This objectivity of thought means that you can learn from all mistakes and find the positive in every negative.

Six in the fourth place means:

At times of great undertakings, it is vital that there is co-operation between all parties concerned. This can be facilitated through the use of an intermediary, but such a person needs to be totally unselfish in their thoughts and deeds, giving benefit to all that need it regardless of rank.

Nine in the fifth place means:

True kindness seeks neither recognition nor reward. Such kindness, because it comes from the heart, will naturally find itself recognized and rewarded, though.

Nine at the top means:

Gentleness of manner and recognition of the needs of others will bring you many allies. Fail to understand this simple truth and you will find yourself alone and vulnerable to attack.

43 Kuai/Breakthrough (Resoluteness)

Above Tui   The Joyous, Lake
Below Ch'ien   The Creative, Heaven

This hexagram is linked to the third month (April–May). It signifies breakthrough as in a river breaking its banks or as a cloud becoming so swollen that it bursts, bringing rain. In terms of human behaviour, it signifies the end of resolute and focused thinking which has led to a positive change in conditions – a breakthrough.

The meaning

For a breakthrough to occur there needs to be a union of energies based upon friendship and honesty. Truth must never be ignored or abandoned in favour of illusion, even if the path of truth at first appears more difficult. Objectivity is essential, you must be aware of your weaknesses and determine to turn them into strengths. Breakthrough will not come through fighting, but through quiet persistence, seeking always that which is good and right.

The image

The image is of the waters of a lake rising towards heaven bringing about the danger of a cloudburst. The warning is not to become so consumed with accumulating energy that you fail to distribute it among those around you. Greed leads only to dissatisfaction and despair. Always examine yourself and your motives. In this way you will remain true both to yourself and to those around you.

The lines

Nine at the beginning means:

When trying to achieve a breakthrough, the initial push forward is the most dangerous time. Do not plunge ahead wildly as this will only lead to failure. Judge the strength of the energies that resist you and allow your strength to accumulate before pressing onwards.

Nine in the second place means:

Be alert and very aware of all the energies that you are attracting into your life. In this way you will not be caught off-guard. You will see danger approaching from afar, will be able to anticipate it and therefore will be free from fear.

Nine in the third place means:

Remain true to yourself, even if that means that those around you misunderstand and misjudge you. The truth will always show in the end and you will ultimately be judged by your actions, not by the words and thoughts of others.

Nine in the fourth place means:

You are trying to press forwards, but are meeting with what appear to be insurmountable obstacles. This is because you are trying to make faster progress than is possible at this time. By obstinately trying to press forwards, you are merely compounding the problem. Stop and think.

Nine in the fifth place means:

To keep a garden free from weeds takes consistent and resolute action. So, too, must you remain focused upon your path, giving consistent effort and never becoming complacent.

Six at the top means:

Success is upon you. Everything appears to be going well and there are just a few minor things to be addressed. There is great danger here because complacency will allow the seeds of misfortune to grow and consume your success. Remain focused and self-examining.

44 Kou/Coming to Meet ☰

Above Ch'ien   The Creative, Heaven
Below Sun   The Gentle, Wind

This hexagram is linked with the fifth month (June–July) and especially to the Summer Solstice. The Summer Solstice is the time after which the nights get longer, the power of the dark 'comes to meet' the power of the light.

The meaning

At this time the power of the dark is small but ever growing. If it is ignored and not dealt with swiftly, it will soon be in danger of consuming you. Just as winter follows summer, this is the way of things and not necessarily 'bad'. The lesson is to remain vigilant and honest at all times.

The image

The image is of the wind blowing under heaven allowing the influence of heaven to be felt upon the earth. The wind blows everywhere, setting things in motion, and in the same way your thoughts and actions can have widespread influence upon those around and beyond you.

The lines

Six at the beginning means:

Weakening influences have wormed their way into your life. It is only by consistent and persistent action that you can avoid bad effects. Allow these influences to grow unchecked and they will bring downfall and misfortune.

Nine in the second place means:

Weakening influences are not repelled by violence, but by gentle, persistent effort. Try to fight them and you will only give them power.

Nine in the third place means:

The only way to avoid danger is to have a clear awareness of it. Guard against complacency.

Nine in the fourth place means:

To make positive use of those around you when you need to, you must not alienate yourself from them, but always remain congenial.

Nine in the fifth place means:

Do not broadcast your understandings to those around you, but let your actions speak for you.

Nine at the top means:

If you distance yourself from the world, the world may misjudge you. This is of no consequence, as by choice of action you will have already learnt how to bear the dislike of others.

45 Ts'ui/Gathering Together (Massing) ䷬

Above Tui   The Joyous, Lake
Below K'un   The Receptive, Earth

This hexagram is related in meaning to Pi, Holding Together (8), which has water above the earth. Here the lake is above the earth, and since a lake is a collecting point for water, the idea of gathering is even more strongly expressed.

The meaning

This is a time of gathering together and a time when much can be achieved. For men to gather together in peace and harmony, they need to be led by someone who has already found peace and harmony within themselves. Such united forces can achieve great things through mutual co-operation and understanding.

The image

The image is of a lake gathering water. There is a danger of the lake gathering too much water and bursting its banks and this should be actively prevented. When there is a gathering of people, there too is a danger of the energy of the people unexpectedly overflowing into conflict. If this is guarded against, all will go well.

The lines

Six at the beginning means:

When people gather together, it is good to have a leader to prevent aimless or misguided wandering. If the people feel they are lost, they can then call out for help and the leader will guide them thus preventing misfortune.

Six in the second place means:

When in a situation of gathering together, it is not good to make solitary decisions but to go with the flow of the group energies.

Six in the third place means:

Often when a man chooses to join with others, he finds that they have already formed a group of which he is outside. To become a part of the core, he must patiently ally himself to someone who is nearer to the core than he is. There is no blame in this.

Nine in the fourth place means:

If you work unselfishly for the good of all, success is assured.

Nine in the fifth place means:

When a leader attracts people to him, not all those people are attracted through honest motives. This situation can be resolved only by the leader gaining the respect and confidence of all through steadfast, unswerving and honest actions.

Six at the top means:

When an individual attempts to ally himself with another, sometimes his actions are misunderstood and he is rejected. This may initially cause pain but that pain may bring about a change of perspective resulting in the union being achieved, so there is no wrong in this.

46 Shêng/Pushing Upward ䷭

Above K'un   The Receptive, Earth
Below Sun   The Gentle, Wind, Wood

This hexagram is similar to Chin, Progress (35) except here the image is of a tree seedling pushing upwards. Progress has an expansive energy, whereas pushing upwards represents a vertical ascent from obscurity to a position of influence.

The meaning

Pushing upwards brings success! Through diligent work and adaptability you can achieve great things. You must have no fear about the path ahead nor about seeking help from others because success is assured.

The image

The image is of a tree growing out of the earth. It grows with neither haste nor rest. It is always moving onwards and upwards, adapting to its ever-changing environment and negotiating obstacles with persistence rather than violence. Learn to embody these energies and nothing will stand in your way.

The lines

Six at the beginning means:

You are at the beginning of a new phase of growth. Step forwards confident in the knowledge that you are naturally forming an affinity with those people who have mastered the lessons that you are now learning, and they in turn will aid your progress.

Nine in the second place means:

You have the resources within you to effect change and if you allow them to grow, external minor failings will not impede you.

Nine in the third place means:

All obstacles on your path are clearing, allowing you to make swift and sure progress. Take advantage of this good fortune. This time will not last for ever but do not spend time wondering how long your good fortune is going to last as this will only waste precious energy.

Six in the fourth place means:

Your efforts are being rewarded. You will gain recognition in all realms and will truly be accepted by your fellows.

Six in the fifth place means:

Do not let success go to your head. You must continue in your efforts steadfastly if you are to achieve your ultimate goal.

Six at the top means:

Pushing upwards blindly only leads to exhaustion. Be diligent and ever mindful of the path ahead, in this way you will continue to make progress.

47 K'un/Oppression (Exhaustion) ䷮

Above Tui   The Joyous, Lake
Below K'an   The Abysmal, Water

When water is below the lake, it can mean only one thing: the lake is dried up. This gives rise to the meaning of oppression and exhaustion.

The meaning

In times of adversity, success is harder to come by but is not impossible. Within every negative is a positive resolution if it can be found. Learn to be like the willow, bend in the wind and as you bend you will find the energy to rebound forwards. Remain inwardly strong and outwardly silent.

The image

The image is of a dried-up lake. The lake has been exhausted of water. This is an act of fate and must be dealt with through steadfastness rather than opposed with violence.

The lines

Six at the beginning means:

In times of adversity it is essential that you find your inner strength and remain true to your path. Do not become downhearted but press ever onwards because little progress is better than no progress at all.

Nine in the second place means:

Although externally things appear fine, inwardly there is turmoil. This situation will be resolved only with patience.

Six in the third place means:

The situation here shows a man who has allowed indecision to get the better of him. He tries to press forwards and is obstructed, he seeks support but there is none, everywhere is disappointment but this is due only to his attitude to the situation. Only a change of perspective can bring resolution.

Nine in the fourth place means:

The situation here shows a man who genuinely wants to help others but begins his efforts with hesitation. This makes the overcoming of obstacles difficult, leading to an inability in the man to fulfil his promises. This in turn causes the man embarrassment, but this is only transitory. Because his intent was good, he will ultimately succeed.

Nine in the fifth place means:

The situation here shows a man who through good intent seeks to help others but is met with opposition from all sides. If he perseveres things will slowly improve.

Six at the top means:

The time of oppression is almost passed. All it takes is a change of attitude and a firm decision, and the whole situation will change from negative to positive.

48 Ching/The Well ☷

Above K'an   The Abysmal, Water
Below Sun   The Gentle, Wind, Wood

The wood is below the water. It has been lowered into the water from above hence the image of a well. There is also the image of a tree's roots descending into the earth to draw water for itself.

The meaning

Dynasties come and go, cities and towns change over the course of time, but the well endures. It nourishes the people without judgment not caring for their political or social standing. The only way it will not give nourishment is if it is not drawn from, or if it is drawn with carelessness. So it is with spiritual nourishment. It is available to everyone and anyone who chooses to take the time and care to draw from it.

The image

The image is twofold; a plant drawing water from the earth and a well, but the message of both images is the same. Just as a plant draws water for the benefit of the whole plant, so too if you nourish yourself by drawing from the well of wisdom, it will benefit not only you, but everyone you meet.

The lines

Six at the beginning means:

If you choose to spend your time in dark places, the nourishment you receive will serve only to weaken you until you become insignificant to all.

Nine in the second place means:

You have many good qualities within you but you are not allowing them to come forth. Continuing in this way will only serve to bring you misfortune.

Nine in the third place means:

This line speaks of a situation where the well is clean and pure, yet no one is choosing to drink from it. If word of its purity could be spread, it would benefit all.

Six in the fourth place means:

There are times when you need to work on yourself and this means that you cannot help others as much but there is no blame in this.

Nine in the fifth place means:

True nourishment can come only when wisdom is taken within and translated into all aspects of life.

Six at the top means:

There is inexhaustible nourishment for all who wish to drink from the well of wisdom.

49 Ko/Revolution (Moulting) ䷰

Above Tui   The Joyous, Lake
Below Li   The Clinging, Fire

Fire and water both try to destroy each other and can be regarded as in conflict, hence the image of revolution. The idea of moulting comes from the seasonal *revolution* that an animal's fur goes through.

The meaning

The only constant is change. In times of revolution, it is only he who acts for the good of the people and is devoid of selfishness and greed who will succeed.

The image

Fire in the lake creates an image of conflict but it can be likened to the ever-changing conflict between light and dark in the unfolding year. If one aligns oneself to the seasons, the conflict causes no problems.

The lines

Nine at the beginning means:

Change should be undertaken only when the time is right. If you proceed too soon, you will only find misfortune.

Six in the second place means:

When all normal avenues of reform have been blocked, revolution becomes the only course of action, but it should be undertaken only with forethought and planning.

Nine in the third place means:

When the time for change comes there are only two possible errors: excessive haste and excessive hesitation. Both will bring misfortune and should be avoided.

Nine in the fourth place means:

To bring about radical changes requires inner strength as well as outward respect from others. If inner motives are not pure and true, there will be no success.

Nine in the fifth place means:

Although you have consulted the oracle, you did not really need to, as the path ahead for you to tread is clear.

Six at the top means:

After fundamental change, there are minor adjustments that need to be made if good fortune is to follow.

50 Ting/The Cauldron ䷱

Above Li   The Clinging, Fire
Below Sun   The Gentle, Wood

This hexagram represents 'The Cauldron' with the bottom line being the legs, the next three lines the belly, the fifth line the handles and the top line the carrying rings. Because in China cauldrons were used for cooking, this hexagram also has the meaning of nourishment. This is similar to Ching, The Well (48) although the latter is more concerned with nourishment of individuals whereas The Cauldron relates to nourishment of the people in general for the benefit of society as a whole.

The meaning

Just as the wood feeds the fire, so we need to seek out those individuals who can fuel our spirit's need for growth. Seeking spiritual nourishment allows us to grow in experience and wisdom and this, in turn, leads to supreme success.

The image

The image is of the cauldron on the cooking fire (fire over wood). Seek true nourishment and your destiny will unfold before you.

The lines

Six at the beginning means:

No matter what is your place in society, if you purify yourself and seek spiritual nourishment there is nothing that you cannot do.

Nine in the second place means:

As you grow in your achievements, you may be a source of envy and jealousy but this will cause you no harm. As you continue to grow, you will naturally distance yourself from such people.

Nine in the third place means:

It appears that all your efforts are for nothing, but do not despair. Recognize that you have deep, spiritual gifts that will, sooner or later, shine through. All will be well.

Nine in the fourth place means:

The task you have taken on is too great for you and you are not putting all your efforts into it. This will lead to failure.

Six in the fifth place means:

You can attract helpers to aid you in your undertakings but you must remain modest and humble if you are to succeed.

Nine at the top means:

Remain gentle and pure and all will go well.

51 Chên/The Arousing (Shock, Thunder) ䷲

Above Chên   The Arousing, Thunder
Below Chên   The Arousing, Thunder

This hexagram has a doubling of the trigram Chên, The Arousing,
Thunder, and represents such a forceful arousing that it sends shock and
terror through the land.

The meaning

The awesome power of creation can strike fear and terror into humankind,
but there is a situation where one is so in tune with nature that one can
remain composed and unmoved by such manifestations. Such a person is
truly powerful.

The image

The image is of continual thunder. At such times it is best to be silent and
to look calmly within to check that you are in balance with nature and at
peace with yourself.

The lines

Nine at the beginning means:

Things appear difficult at present but this is only transitory. The anguish
you now feel will soon be turned to joy.

Six in the second place means:

This is a time for letting go. It appears that you are losing many things,
but once you learn acceptance of loss, you will gain everything back and
more.

Six in the third place means:

Shock can be a good thing especially if it stirs one's mind into action and
thus creates movement.

Nine in the fourth place means:

This is a time when movement in any direction is prevented.

Six in the fifth place means:

You are being subjected to shock after shock and you must remain centred
if you are to resist being tossed around by fate.

Six at the top means:

Inner shock caused by witnessing a trauma can rob one of clarity of thought. When those around you are being subjected to misfortune, the correct course of action is to withdraw and do nothing until clarity is restored within you.

52 Kên/Keeping Still, Mountain

Above Kên   **Keeping Still, Mountain**
Below Kên   **Keeping Still, Mountain**

This hexagram represents the mountain. The idea of stillness comes from the construction of the trigram Kên. The top, yang line and the bottom two yin lines are in a state of mutual attraction and repulsion. They embody a state of dynamic equilibrium. In relation to man, the lesson of this hexagram is that one can truly find inner stillness (peace) only when one is truly balanced.

The meaning

True peace comes from knowing when to be still and when to move forwards. In this way the balance between yin and yang is maintained. When one learns peace, one masters the ego. This allows for true objectivity and non-judgment of others.

The image

The image is of mountains standing together and conveying the idea of constancy. True constancy comes from learning to live always in the present. The past is just a memory, the future just a dream, here and now is the only place where you can have true influence.

The lines

Six at the beginning means:

This line refers to a person who stops before they have even begun something. At the outset of any endeavour, early mistakes can cost dear. If you are cautious, provided you do not abandon your goal, there is no mistake in this.

Six in the second place means:

If you sense danger, do not allow the onward motion of others to carry you forwards into it.

Nine in the third place means:

Peace cannot be found through force but rather needs to be cultivated by quieting the mind and learning to accept everything with pleasure.

Six in the fourth place means:

This line refers to a situation where a man has control of his ego at present but has not truly mastered it. Although this is not the ultimate goal, this temporary mastering can allow positive energies to develop.

Six in the fifth place means:

Words are energy. Be careful not to speak frivolously and without due thought.

Nine at the top means:

This line indicates ultimate peace where a man has truly mastered his ego and can view all matters with clarity and objectivity.

53 Chien/Development (Gradual Progress) ䷴

Above Sun   The Gentle, Wind, Wood
Below Kên   Keeping Still, Mountain

The tree on the mountainside grows and develops slowly but puts down firm roots. This conveys the lesson that to truly achieve something, each part of the process needs to unfold step by step with each phase being completed before the next one is begun.

The meaning

As you go through life, for you to develop to your true potential, you must proceed one step at a time, learning each lesson that life brings you. Every lesson must be truly mastered for you to make sure progress. Although it seems that things are moving slowly, you must persevere onwards or you will find yourself at a standstill.

The image

The image is of a tree growing on the side of a mountain. It is visible from afar and as it develops, so it changes and influences the surrounding landscape. Its progress is slow but sure and its roots run deep. This is how you need to proceed, through constancy and careful persistence.

The lines

Six at the beginning means:

Each line of this hexagram symbolizes the process by which a wild goose attains flight. The goose is symbolic of fidelity, as it was believed that wild geese mate for life and that if a mate died, its partner never sought another mate. Here the goose is still on the ground at rest. It has not yet taken its first steps towards flight and so is vulnerable, but this is far preferable to hasty flight into danger so there is no blame in waiting.

Six in the second place means:

Here the goose gradually draws to the edge of the cliff. The cliff symbolizes safety and security, and movement forwards is positive as it symbolizes the overcoming of initial insecurities.

Nine in the third place means:

Here the goose is on the plateau, a place that is not suited to it and full of potential danger. It symbolizes the man who steps forwards into danger through rashness rather than allowing things to unfold at a gentle pace.

Six in the fourth place means:

Here the goose is in a tree, which is not its favourite resting place although if it finds a flat branch it will be able to rest safely. This symbolizes the man who, despite finding himself in the wrong place, has the opportunity to find safety from surrounding dangers.

Nine in the fifth place means:

Here the goose is at the summit of the mountain, a place of isolation but also a place from where it can fly to freedom. This symbolizes the man who finds himself in a position of isolation where others do not understand him. He should not be downcast, though, as this place offers him a route to freedom and fulfilment.

Nine at the top means:

Here the goose is flying heavenwards leaving the world behind. This symbolizes the completion of something. It is the time to leave what is completed behind and press onwards towards new enlightenments.

54 Kuei Mei/The Marrying Maiden ䷵

Above Chên   The Arousing, Thunder
Below Tui   The Joyous, Lake

In this hexagram Chên, the eldest son is above with Tui, the youngest daughter below. This depicts the attraction between a mature young man and an innocent maiden whom he marries, hence the hexagram title, the marrying maiden.

The meaning

In ancient Chinese society, when a maiden married a man, she entered the household of the man's family in subjugation to the mistress of the household. If she tried to usurp the female head of the household, it would lead to disharmony and would jeopardize her relationship with her man. This means that in relationships with others, you must not overstep the boundaries of that relationship and cause disharmony.

The image

The image is of thunder stirring up water and causing waves. If you are to have enduring relationships, you need to be ever mindful that there will always be challenges to that relationship either from outside sources or from misunderstandings and miscommunications within the relationship itself. The only way to counteract this is to be aware of these dangers and to avert them so that the waves do not dash the relationship on the rocks.

The lines

Nine at the beginning means:

No matter what your place in life, if you harmonize with those around you, you can make good progress.

Nine in the second place means:

Even if others let you down, do not let this change your loyalty to those whom you love.

Six in the third place means:

Sometimes to achieve great heights, one needs to begin from a lowly position.

Nine in the fourth place means:

Be patient, do not compromise your dream and it will reach fulfilment.

Six in the fifth place means:

You need to adapt to changing circumstances. If you concentrate on inner change, good fortune will follow.

Six at the top means:

Superficial actions will achieve nothing. It is only through hard work and integrity that you will succeed.

55 Fêng/Abundance (Fullness) ䷶

Above Chên   The Arousing, Thunder
Below Li   The Clinging, Fire

Chên represents external movement, while Li represents internal clarity. When these two energies combine, it represents the peak of achievement, hence the hexagram's title of Abundance.

The meaning

This is a time of great abundance and good fortune that will inevitably be followed by a period of decline. The wise person does not look forward with sorrow to the time of decline, but lives in the present and takes full advantage of the prevailing conditions while they last.

The image

The image is of thunder and lightning together and is linked to the hexagram Shih Ho, Biting Through (21) where the same two elements appear in reverse order. Shih Ho lays down the laws for overcoming an obstruction whereas Fêng applies those laws.

The lines

Nine at the beginning means:

A union between clarity and movement brings about a time of abundance. This union can last during the whole time of abundance and there will be no wrong in this, for it will bring you recognition.

Six in the second place means:

Hold on to the truth within you, even if all around you are living in illusion. In this way you will exert an invisible, yet highly beneficial influence and all will go well.

Nine in the third place means:

In a time of abundance, even the most insignificant people can push to the foreground of affairs and may even temporarily halt your progress, but there is no blame in this.

Nine in the fourth place means:

You must use your wisdom to take full advantage of this time of abundance.

Six in the fifth place means:

In this time of good fortune, do not let arrogance prevent you from listening to the counsel of others. Through co-operation and understanding, great things can be achieved to the benefit of all.

Six at the top means:

This line describes a man who has allowed arrogance to cloud his judgement. He has sought external splendour and in doing so, has alienated all those whom he has regarded as friends. This brings loneliness and misfortune.

56 Lü/The Wanderer ☲

Above Li   The Clinging, Fire
Below Kên   Keeping Still, Mountain

Here the fire is above the mountain and has nothing to feed it so the two energies part, bringing the idea of separation. In the same way, the wanderer separates himself from society and wanders in strange lands.

The meaning

The path of the wanderer is a lonely path. He must rely upon his own integrity to keep him focused in his path and should be devoid of airs and arrogance towards those he meets on his path. He should seek the company of good people and walk away from potential danger. In this way he will make sure progress.

The image

The image is of fire on the mountain. When grass catches fire on a mountain, it burns with a bright flame yet tarries not in one place, but moves ever onwards in search of new fuel. This teaches that you must never allow yourself to become stagnant, but should be ever moving onwards and upwards.

The lines

Six at the beginning means:

Do not become waylaid by trivialities but maintain your integrity and inner dignity.

Six in the second place means:

By maintaining your inner clarity, you will attract good and honest help upon your path.

Nine in the third place means:

Be very wary of becoming involved in matters that do not concern you as this will lead to danger.

Nine in the fourth place means:

Draw upon your inner strength while being on guard to any potential dangers on your unfolding path.

Six in the fifth place means:

If you treat those whom you meet with honour and respect, you will attract many friends and allies.

Nine at the top means:

Guard against losing your integrity through foolish behaviour or you may lose sight of your path.

57 Sun/The Gentle (The Penetrating, Wind) ☴

Above Sun The Gentle, Wind, Wood
Below Sun The Gentle, Wind, Wood

The attributes of both wind and wood are gentle yet penetrating. The wind blows into every corner and the roots of a tree gently but firmly penetrate the earth.

The meaning

Gentleness and persistence, rather than force and violence, will allow you to make sure progress. Although less dynamic than a sudden attack, this kind of action will allow you to have a more permanent and lasting effect provided that you have a clear intent of the direction in which you wish to proceed.

The image

The image is of unceasing wind exerting strong influence over time, and teaches persistence of thought and action. This signifies a time when great things can be achieved, but this can become reality only through careful planning and by clearly defining your goal.

The lines

Six at the beginning means:

Gentleness can sometimes lead to irresolute action. The mind is full of doubts and fears leading to a situation where one is tossed to and fro. The only right course of action is to be decisive.

Nine in the second place means:

You must seek out the root cause of all negative influences if you are to be free from them.

Nine in the third place means:

Do not become so embroiled in pondering matters that you spend all your time thinking and no time acting. Once you have thoroughly thought about an issue, take resolute action or new doubts and fears will arise.

Six in the fourth place means:

If you remain humble while pressing onwards you will achieve success.

Nine in the fifth place means:

Although things have not started well, you now have an opportunity to take a new direction that will bring improvement. This opportunity must be taken with thought and consideration at every stage of its unfolding if good fortune is to be achieved.

Nine at the top means:

The time for advancement has ended and any fight against dark influences will bring misfortune. Better to withdraw and renew your strength.

58 Tui/The Joyous, Lake ䷹

Above Tui   The Joyous, Lake
Below Tui   The Joyous, Lake

The doubling of the trigram Tui symbolizes a time of joyousness which is founded upon inner strength.

The meaning

True joy is infectious and endures because it is founded upon inner strength. Without this strength, joy degenerates into uncontrolled frivolity. Actively seek those things in your life that make you happy, healthy and fulfilled and success and joy will both be yours.

The image

A single lake may dry up, but when two lakes are together, they each feed one another and so the dangers of them drying up are greatly lessened. So it is with knowledge: learning should be stimulating and enjoyable with each new experience feeding your pool of knowledge. Everything you encounter is an opportunity to learn and should be embraced with pleasure.

The lines

Nine at the beginning means:

True joy comes from within and is not dependent upon other people or circumstances. Such joy brings freedom and good fortune.

Nine in the second place means:

We too often seek joy in external pleasures rather than finding it within ourselves, and this can lead to disappointment and dissatisfaction. If we recognize the futility of such action and resolve to find true joy, good fortune will follow.

Six in the third place means:

If one has no inner joy, worldly pleasures can fill the void which will bring dissatisfaction, instability and misfortune.

Nine in the fourth place means:

You are presented with a choice of worldly or spiritual pleasures and you will not have inner peace until you choose wisely. Worldly pleasures do not bring lasting joy. By choosing to turn away from such low pleasures and by actively seeking higher pleasures, you will achieve joy, success and inner peace.

Nine in the fifth place means:

Temptation comes to every man and if allowed to remain within the mind, will only serve to attract misfortune. Recognize the danger, protect yourself from it and you will remain free from harm.

Six at the top means:

This describes a situation where, through inner weakness, a man has allowed himself to be swept along by worldly pleasures. He has lost control of his life and has become a victim of fate.

59 Huan/Dispersion (Dissolution) ䷺

Above Sun   The Gentle, Wind
Below K'an   The Abysmal, Water

The gentle wind blowing upon the water disperses it. This symbolizes a man who has an internal energy block that can be broken up and dispersed through gentleness rather than force.

The meaning

When men unite in mutual co-operation, any barrier can be overcome. This can be achieved only by men who are free from selfish influences and understand the need to work for the good of all rather than purely for the self. In such undertakings, the ego must be truly mastered for success to be assured.

The image

The image is of the warm spring winds gently dissolving the frozen winter lakes, bringing fluidity and movement where there was once rigidity. This relates to the ego of man. A powerful ego brings only stubbornness and rigidity as it breeds selfishness and hardness towards others. Through gentleness of the heart, the ego can be mastered and the emotions no longer remain suppressed.

The lines

Six at the beginning means:

When there are the beginnings of misunderstandings and disharmony between individuals, they must be resolved quickly and efficiently for good fortune to prevail.

Nine in the second place means:

If you find yourself becoming alienated from others, you must actively seek within yourself the cause and correct it.

Six in the third place means:

Sometimes a difficult task requires a level of self-sacrifice if success is to be achieved and there is no remorse in this.

Six in the fourth place means:

When working for the good of all, you must not allow personal friendships to cloud your judgement and prevent you from doing that which you know is right.

Nine in the fifth place means:

At times of deadlock, a great idea can relieve the blockage and give all parties a focal point from which they can initiate movement.

Nine at the top means:

If you see approaching danger, you must warn those around you rather than merely seeking to save yourself. In this way you will do what is right and all will benefit.

60 Chieh/Limitation ䷻

Above K'an   The Abysmal, Water
Below Tui   The Joyous, Lake

The lake has its boundaries and when more water is added to it, it overflows. To prevent this from happening, stronger boundaries need setting up, hence the idea of limitation. Limitation prevents things running out of control. In general life it refers to being prudent and setting limits upon your expenditure whether it is financial, emotional or energetic. In the spiritual realm it refers to setting limits upon your thinking in such a way as to prevent you becoming side-tracked by unimportant issues.

The meaning

Setting limitations is a necessary, but difficult task because there is a fine line between limiting your expenditure and creating restriction. To be prudent with your expenditure of energy prevents you from over-stretching your resources and also prepares you for times of hardship when your energies are low. This can apply to financial, emotional, spiritual or physical energies, but if the limitation becomes overly restrictive, then ill-health will result so one must even put limitations on the level of limitation.

The image

There are two images here, the lake and water. The lake provides the image of limitations whereas water is inexhaustible. In life there are limitless possibilities yet without setting yourself boundaries, you will achieve nothing. Decide where your energies should best be used and where they are being wasted. Seek only those things that make you happy, healthy and fulfilled. This can be achieved only through honest self-examination.

The lines

Nine at the beginning means:

You are confronted by seemingly insurmountable limitations. If you try to press forwards, you will only waste your energy. It is better to stop, wait and accumulate your energies until the time is right for you to use that stored energy to press forwards.

Nine in the second place means:

Now is the time for action. The obstacles have been removed and to hesitate will only bring misfortune.

Six in the third place means:

If you are bent upon seeking only pleasures and excitement, you may lose your sense of limitation and overspend your energies. If this occurs, it is entirely your responsibility and not the fault of others. Once you understand this truth you will be able to avoid this situation.

Six in the fourth place means:

Limitation is only valuable when it saves energy. If enforcing limitation depletes energy, then it is pointless. Some limitations are natural (such as gravity) and can be harnessed so as to save energy. On a spiritual level understanding of the laws of the universe brings understanding of the limitations that can be harnessed to help you on your path.

Nine in the fifth place means:

If you are to put limitations upon others, you must first put limitations upon yourself if you are to avoid anger and resentment. Lead by example and all will go well.

Six at the top means:

To apply ruthless, persistent limitations upon yourself or others is unhealthy and will lead to disharmony. There are times, however, when short-term, hard restriction can be of benefit (e.g. fasting).

61 Chung Fu/Inner Truth ䷼

Above Sun **The Gentle, Wind**
Below Tui **The Joyous, Lake**

The invisible wind blows on the lake and creates visible effects. So it is with inner truth because although it cannot be seen, its effects are manifest for all to see. The truth will always ultimately shine forth.

The meaning

To exert a positive influence upon others, one must first cultivate inner truth and become devoid of prejudice. Once this is established, one must then find the right approach with which to communicate these truths to others. If you can find the correct way to 'connect' with another person, even the most hardened and stubborn individuals can be positively influenced.

The image

The image is of the wind penetrating the lake and thus causing movement. In the same manner, you need to penetrate the minds of others in order to convey truths to them.

The lines

Nine at the beginning means:

To be able to convey inner truths is dependent upon the stability of your mind and inner being and not dependent upon your relationships with others. If you rely too much upon others, you are in danger of losing the force behind your inner truth and will not be able to effectively convey it to others nor utilize it for yourself.

Nine in the second place means:

If you speak and act with honesty and truth, your influence will be felt by many even when you are not in the forefront of things.

Six in the third place means:

If you rely too much upon others, you will be a victim of fate, powerless to exert influence on your own life and to seek that which makes you happy, healthy and fulfilled.

Six in the fourth place means:

To learn inner truths from others requires humility and openness, but this has to be balanced with a strong and straight purpose if you are to reach your goal.

Nine in the fifth place means:

Only when your inner truth is so strong that it shines forth in your personality can you truly unite others to your cause.

Nine at the top means:

Do not rely upon your words to awaken the truth in others; your actions will speak louder and with more power.

62 Hsiao Kuo/Preponderance of the Small ䷽

Above Chên   The Arousing, Thunder
Below Kên   Keeping Still, Mountain

Although the core of this hexagram contains two strong lines, the external lines are all weak. This symbolizes a situation where a man attains a place of authority for which he is poorly suited and must exercise extreme prudence if he is not to jeopardize his core strength.

The meaning

Modesty and hard work are rewarded with success but you must guard against getting carried away. Remain grounded and consolidate your success. If you try to strive ever higher without consolidating, you will find all your plans come to nothing.

The image

The image is of thunder on the mountain signifying a need for caution and conscientiousness. Let prudence and simplicity be your watchwords. This manner will seem exceptional to others but is the only correct way to act in the present situation. Give your attention to internal rather than external matters.

The lines

Six at the beginning means:

Do not try to run before you can walk or all your efforts will amount to nothing.

Six in the second place means:

Remain modest and conscientious in all your works.

Nine in the third place means:

Although you are right, you must guard against arrogance and pride. You must be especially vigilant against attack or you will be caught off-guard and will pay painful consequences.

Nine in the fourth place means:

Extreme caution is called for. Do not try to press forwards towards your goal but concentrate upon strengthening your inner resolve.

Six in the fifth place means:

To reach your goal you need to enlist the help of others. When seeking such help, you should look at people's actions rather than relying upon their reputations, and in this way you will be able to make wise choices.

Six at the top means:

Do not try to press ever onwards at this time, as it will result in you missing your goal. Learn when it is the right time to move and the right time to rest.

63 Chi Chi/After Completion ䷾

Above K'an   The Abysmal, Water
Below Li   The Clinging, Fire

This hexagram signifies a time when chaos has turned to order and everything is in its correct place. Although this is a very positive hexagram, it also describes a need for great caution because if the wrong movement is undertaken, the situation can easily dissolve into chaos once more.

The meaning

The time of transition is already complete and everything is in order, but this does not mean that you should relax and rest on your laurels. On the contrary, it is only by remaining ever vigilant that success can continue.

The image

Water over fire gives the image of the kettle being boiled over the fire. If the fire is too hot, all the water evaporates. On the other hand, if the kettle boils over, it extinguishes the fire. It is only through vigilance and caution that such misfortune can be avoided. At this time when everything is in harmony and order, you must be aware of all the potential dangers and threats to that order if it is to be maintained.

The lines

Nine at the beginning means:

After a time of transition everything is moving onwards and upwards but forcibly pressing forwards would be a mistake. Do not let yourself become taken up by the general feeling of positivity, but remain centred and allow things to unfold at their own pace. In this way you will remain free from blame.

Six in the second place means:

Do not seek recognition at this time but keep developing your inner worth. Times change and if you are patient and humble recognition will come.

Nine in the third place means:

After a time of transition comes a time of expansion when new ideas and thoughts are expressed. At such times, this expansion can lead to conflict as those around you resist change but this is the natural way of things when ambitious ideas are undertaken.

Six in the fourth place means:

During change, negative things can be brought to the fore and because the general feeling is one of peace and harmony they can tend to be glossed over and forgotten. You would be wise to heed such things as omens and remain guarded as this will keep you from danger.

Nine in the fifth place means:

During times of change and expansion, the simple can become ever more elaborate and complicated. Do not get caught up in such developments. Keep everything simple and you will get your just reward.

Six at the top means:

Having overcome danger and perils, you must not look back but press onwards without pausing. Looking back over past perils will only put you into further danger.

64 Wei Chi/Before Completion ☲☵

Above Li   The Clinging, Fire
Below K'an   The Abysmal, Water

This hexagram describes a situation where the transition from chaos to order is underway but not yet complete. The previous hexagram can be likened to autumn as the transition from summer to winter. Here the hexagram can be likened to spring which leads out of the stagnation of the winter months into the summer, a time of growth and fruition. It is with this positive outlook that the *Book of Changes* draws to a close.

The meaning

This is a time of great difficulty and responsibility as you draw order out of chaos but the future looks bright and your goal is totally achievable. You must be cautious, though, as the time of potential danger is not yet fully over and you could easily get drawn back into chaos.

The image

The image is of fire over water. The flames of fire move upwards while water flows downwards so that the two energies do not meet. For you to change this situation to one of balance and harmony, you must remain objective and view the situation from a perspective of balance and internal harmony.

The lines

Six at the beginning means:

In times of disorder, there is a temptation to press forwards in the hope of advancing beyond the danger but this will only lead to misfortune. The time for advancement has not yet arrived and your best action is to remain still and consolidate your energies so that when the time for advancement does arrive, you are ready and able to take full advantage of it.

Nine in the second place means:

Again the time for advancement has not yet arrived but in this situation you must not wait idly for change to come to you. You must strengthen yourself so that you are strong enough to move forwards when the time is right. Be patient and ever watchful and all will go well.

Six in the third place means:

The time for movement has come but you lack the strength to take advantage of it. Trying to force yourself forwards will only lead to failure. Seek the help of others and together you will be able to achieve your goal.

Nine in the fourth place means:

The time of transition has been initiated but you will need to use all your strength and energies to bring it to completion. Do not allow doubts and fears to take you away from your focus but silence them in your mind and you will reap your just reward.

Six in the fifth place means:

Everything has been overcome and all is well. This signifies a time when the sun shines after the rains have finished and heralds a new dawn of positivity.

Nine at the top means:

At the dawning of a new era of positivity, there is cause for friends to gather together and celebrate and there is no blame in this. However, one must guard against over-indulgence, as this will bring humiliation.

The *Book of Changes* ends at the point Before Completion representing the transition from chaos to order and showing that at the end there is always a new beginning. Thus the *Book of Changes* ends on a note of hope for the future.

Key to the hexagrams

Trigram Upper → Lower ↓	☰ Ch'ien	☳ Chên	☵ K'an	☶ Kên	☷ K'un	☴ Sun	☲ Li	☱ Tui
☰ Ch'ien	1	34	5	26	11	9	14	43
☳ Chên	25	51	3	27	24	42	21	17
☵ K'an	6	40	29	4	7	59	64	47
☶ Kên	33	62	39	52	15	53	56	31
☷ K'un	12	16	8	23	2	20	35	45
☴ Sun	44	32	48	18	46	57	50	28
☲ Li	13	55	63	22	36	37	30	49
☱ Tui	10	54	60	41	19	61	38	58

FURTHER READING

I Ching or *Book of Changes*, trans. Richard Wilhelm (Arkana 1989)

The Essential Ohsawa, George Ohsawa (Avery Publishing 1994)

Traditional Chinese Medicine, Daniel Reid (Shambhala 1996)

The Zen Teachings of Master Lin-Chi, trans. Burton Watson (Shambhala 1993)

The Five Houses of Zen, Thomas Cleary (Shambhala 1997)

Road to Heaven (Encounters with Chinese Hermits), Bill Porter (Mercury House 1993)

The Power of Chi, Michael Page (Aquarian 1988)

Zen in the Art of Archery, Eugen Herrigel (Arkana 1985)

Tao The Watercourse Way, Alan Watts (Penguin 1979)

Tao Te Ching-Lao Tzu, trans. Richard Wilhelm (Arkana 1990)

Chinese Medicine The Web that has no Weaver, Ted J. Kaptchuk (Rider 1985)

INDEX

The name of each hexagram is followed by its number, in parentheses.

TEACH YOURSELF

FENG SHUI

Richard Craze & Roni Jay

Feng Shui is the ancient Chinese art of arranging your surroundings to receive maximum benefit from good 'ch'i' – universal energy. In *Teach Yourself Feng Shui* the authors explain in a clear and practical way how this popular subject can be learnt and utilised at home, at work and in the garden.

The book covers:

- the history and principles of Feng Shui
- the practical application of Feng Shui
- how to use Feng Shui to influence your relationships, money, health and children.

Richard Craze and Roni Jay are both professional writers for various subjects including New Age and Alternative Health and they have written extensively on Feng Shui.

TEACH YOURSELF

TAI CHI

Robert Parry

Tai chi is a centuries-old system of exercise from China which is gaining increasing popularity in the West. The movements flow into one another in a slow, graceful pattern and are suitable for all ages and levels of fitness.

This richly illustrated book explains the basics of tai chi and contains step-by-step instructions for learning the Short Yang Form – a sequence of gentle exercise that takes only eight minutes to complete. Daily practice promotes relaxation and well-being and increases levels of concentration and personal creativity. Tai chi is the perfect antidote to the stressful life of today.

Robert Parry has a life-long interest in the health and relaxation aspects of Eastern systems of exercise. He is a qualified shiatsu practitioner and an experienced teacher of tai chi.

TEACH YOURSELF

VISUALIZATION

Pauline Wills

Visualization, the carrying of a clear visual image in the mind, has long been accepted in the East as playing an important role in balancing and maintaining the mind-body-spirit relationship.

This book will show you how to practice the techniques, using simple, clearly illustrated exercises, to relieve stress, alleviate specific health problems and increase your sense of well-being – in your personal relationships, at work, and in all aspects of your everyday life. The book includes a selection of mandalas which you can use in your request for personal growth.

Pauline Wills first trained as a nurse. She subsequently developed an interest in complementary therapies, and now uses visualization alongside a wide range of other treatments. She has written extensively on reflexology and colour therapy.

ty TEACH YOURSELF

MEDITATION

Naomi Ozaniec

Meditation is a traditional discipline which has been practised through the ages, and has long been recognised for its spiritual and restorative powers.

Teach Yourself Meditation introduces the theory and practice of meditation in a direct and simple manner. The book includes a variety of approaches, and compares the methods and goals of both Eastern and Western systems. With its holistic view of life, meditation can help you to gain a new perspective for the future.

Naomi Ozaniec has studied meditation for over ten years and has written several books on the subject.

Other related titles

ALTERNATIVE MEDICINE

Loulou Brown

This practical and safe reference book gives invaluable information on the uses and benefits of both complementary and alternative therapies. With an A–Z of over 50 therapies, and explanations of how to stay healthy with the right therapy, the book provides an essential guide for anyone wanting to find out more about this fast-growing branch of medicine. In addition, a list of conditions and appropriate therapies for treatment of these conditions is included.

From acupuncture, colour therapy and flower remedies to reiki, visualization and yoga, this book gives a well-balanced and comprehensive look at available therapies and how to get the best from them.

Loulou Brown is a writer with a special interest in complementary and alternative medicine. Her first book on the subject, *Working in Complementary and Alternative Medicine*, was published in 1994.

Other related titles

TEACH YOURSELF

CHINESE ASTROLOGY

Richard Craze *with* Billy Lee

Teach Yourself Chinese Astrology is a clear and practical guide which explains how this ancient and well-tested system of astrology works. The basic idea is that people are classified according to certain fundamental types, which are described by twelve animals and relate to the year of birth. This book will show you how to construct and interpret your own personal and unique Chinese astrological charts, as well as the charts of your friends and family.

Not only can you find out what animal you are and what it means in Chinese astrology, but you can also discover your secret animal and how it can help you improve your career, relationships, health and luck. Whether you are a dragon, a monkey or a snake by birth year, it is certain that you are never just one animal, but a combination of several – the fascinating part is finding out which ones!

Richard Craze is a freelance writer, specializing in books on Chinese culture, the New Age and religion. Billy Lee is a Chinese astrologer and Tai Ch'i teacher.